Animals Make Us Human

Animals Make Us Human

Edited by

Leah Kaminsky & Meg Keneally

Supporting

Australian Marine Conservation Society
& Australian Wildlife Conservancy

PENGUIN LIFE

UK | USA | Canada | Ireland | Australia
India | New Zealand | South Africa | China

Penguin Life is part of the Penguin Random House group of companies whose addresses can be
found at global.penguinrandomhouse.com

Penguin
Random House
Australia

First published by Penguin Life in 2020

'Garrall' from *Bindi* by Kirli Saunders reproduced by permission of Magabala Books.

'Sleep, Australia, Sleep', written by Paul Kelly, reproduced by permission of Sony/ATV Music
Publishing (Australia) Pty Limited. International copyright secured. All rights reserved.

Photographs by Caleb McElrea reproduced by permission of Caleb McElrea Media.

Cover photography by Kristian Bell

Cover design by James Rendall © Penguin Random House Australia Pty Ltd

Photograph of Leah Kaminsky by Karen Quist; photograph of Meg Keneally by Lee Hulsman,
Summerland Photography

Illustrations and internal design by James Rendall

Typeset in Optima LT Pro by James Rendall, Penguin Random House Australia

Printed and bound in China by R. R. Donnelley

 A catalogue record for this
book is available from the
National Library of Australia

ISBN 978 1 76089 981 3

penguin.com.au

MIX
Paper from
responsible sources
FSC® C144853

For the contributors who gave their time and talent to this book.
For our families.
And for the animals.

—LK and MK

The animals in this book have been on the Earth for far longer than the society that now threatens their existence. They have walked and swum alongside First Nations communities for millennia. The editors would like to acknowledge the Traditional Owners of the land, waters and skies in which these animals live, and pay their respects to Elders past, present and emerging who have and will always care for them.

Contents

Foreword

From Bruce Pascoe

Sometimes I look at my dogs, their furry, clawy feet, their silly noses, their ridiculous tails, and I think, why? Why does a creature so different from me watch my every move, and why do I watch every move of theirs? Why do they smile so gooily at me in the morning, why in the dark of night do I smile so deeply when I hear them sigh? How can we, two such different forms of life, devote ourselves so completely to each other?

They could leave at any moment, but they don't. When the dingoes call on the other side of the river, they cock their ears for a moment but then go back to sleep. Why are we together? It is true that we have removed some primary functions and motivations from their lives, but they could both swim the river, they do it often enough. Yet they don't, they shut their eyes and squirm closer into our three-body plait.

We all crowd onto the same couch in front of the fire, shuffling and pushing until the assemblage accommodates six hips, ten legs, two tails and three heads. Why is it such bliss?

If I am sick, even though this happens rarely, why is it that one of my dogs chooses to place himself so that we face each other and he breathes his warm nuttiness directly onto my face, and she, terribly intimidated by her bossy brother, takes second position on the grid behind my knees?

We ought to be anathemas to each other, but we are not. The strangeness of a dog's face should separate us as species but instead we kiss them between the eyes, and they squirm with delight. Why?

I think it is because we are fellow creatures and at a level deeper than our own ego we recognise the dignity of their life. If a pelican turns to look at me, if a king parrot swivels an eye towards me if I sneeze, if a scrubwren gets excited if I pick up a shovel, there is a delight in my soul which is unmatched. If a night heron stalks behind me while I am fishing at midnight, a volcanic astonishment thrills in me; I have been ignored by an animal, counted as an equal, so similar are our occupations.

None of these animals can open a can of baked beans, but that is the very least of our disparity. We are fellow creatures and notice each other. If only humans could show the same respect for the differences in our species.

From the editors

_____

As children, most of us feel an instinctive affection for animals. But as we grow, many of us lose this strong tie to nature.

We believe that those who form an emotional connection with our native wildlife are more likely to work to protect it. That is why, in this book, we chose to explore our human connection with animals. Each contributor has written about a species or ecosystem with which they have forged a strong bond.

We felt the best way of encouraging an appreciation of Australia's unique animals was to allow readers to hear about them from people who are already in love, and to see them through the lenses of photographers who feel that deep connection as well.

This book was conceived after Australia's devastating bushfires in the summer of 2019–20 and put together during the COVID-19 pandemic that followed. Both events were tragedies. One of them was a tragedy shared with the animals who inhabit this country alongside us. The bushfires were the latest in a string of insults to the environment that supports our wildlife – habitat destruction, introduced species, and the warming oceans and more frequent natural disasters brought about by climate change are all sources of immense pressure, all threats to their survival, and ours.

The fires were a call to action, underscoring the fragility of our precious ecosystems and what is at risk of being lost. We pulled this book together during the pandemic isolation period, when people stuck at home longed to be outside again, surrounded by nature. Yet this period also gave many the opportunity to appreciate the nature that surrounds us – birds, beetles and butterflies in our backyards and nature strips – that we tend to overlook in the busyness of our daily lives.

Animals Make Us Human has two goals. The first is to raise money for the Australian Marine Conservation Society and Australian Wildlife Conservancy, both of which do invaluable work for wildlife and habitat conservation. The second is to highlight the vulnerability of Australia's distinctive terrestrial and marine wildlife in the face of climate change and other threats.

In this book you will find a range of perspectives, from professional wildlife researchers to well-known writers, telling their stories of connection and reflecting on their relationship with nature. As you'll see, when people write about animals, their humanity, love and compassion come to the fore.

We hope this book reminds you of what you love about our unique wildlife and inspires you to help protect it. This is why we are donating all proceeds from this collection to the AMCS and AWC. Like us, the writers and photographers who have contributed were not paid for sharing their work. We are indebted to every one of them, and we hope you, the reader, will find a deeper connection with our extraordinary wildlife through their words and images.

—*Leah Kaminsky and Meg Keneally*

From Australian Wildlife Conservancy

There's something awe-inspiring about returning a regionally extinct animal to its former home. The moment when it takes its first steps (usually followed by a giant leap) on the land where its ancestors once lived in abundance is a moment when we can celebrate healing our land, and righting our wrongs.

This is something that Australian Wildlife Conservancy has the privilege of doing around the country. Our fundamental mission is to protect all Australian native animals and their habitats. Considering the size of the continent, it's a big task. But it's worth it. We protect some of the last remaining populations of Australia's most threatened species at our sanctuaries, and also in partnership with governments, landholders and other conservation groups.

Australia is one of only seventeen 'mega-diverse' countries on the planet. Much of our unique fauna and flora cannot be found anywhere else on Earth.

For tens of thousands of years, Indigenous Australians were custodians of this country – maintaining practices that ensured the survival of species, such as the platypus, the numbat and the iconic koala.

Today, unfortunately, we hold the record for the worst mammal extinction rate on the planet, and we have also lost (and continue to lose) many species of reptiles, amphibians, birds and plants. In the centuries since Europeans set foot in Australia, we have lost more than thirty mammal species. This extinction rate is not slowing down; rather, it is accelerating. We now have fifty mammal species at risk of extinction in the coming decade. Once gone, they are gone forever.

This extinction rate is largely driven by the influence of European settlement. Early settlers introduced animals that disturbed the ecological balance. Feral cats and foxes feast on species that have no defence against introduced predators. Rabbits compete for habitat and vegetation, further contracting the range of animals like the bilby that once covered more than 75 per cent of the Australian continent.

These settlers also oversaw a radical change in fire management across the landscape through the elimination of Indigenous practices, and completely misguided attempts to apply European landcare practices.

With numerous species already at risk, the bushfires during the summer of 2019–20 pushed many to the brink. A catastrophe of this magnitude forces us to consider what it is we value about our distinctive Australian wildlife. The fires in south-east Australia were a devastating but long overdue wake-up call to the grim future many species will face if we do not act now.

Australian Wildlife Conservancy has taken on the challenge to act to secure a future for this country's native species. As you read the stories in this book, I ask you to consider what it is you value about Australia and its wildlife, and what actions you can take. Together, we can make sure that tomorrow will be better than today for all of us, and for our unique wildlife. It's not too late.

—Tim Allard, CEO, Australian Wildlife Conservancy

Australians have a deep bond with the ocean. As inhabitants of an island continent, it is our great privilege to grow up surrounded by coasts and seas with such amazing diversity of life and colour.

But that diversity is under threat. Global studies have revealed that our northern oceans are some of the last remaining healthy tropical seas in the world. An incredible 80 per cent of the marine species found in our cool southern oceans occur nowhere else on earth.

This means that if we lose them from our waters, they will be lost from the world forever.

Australians love dolphins, seals and sea turtles, but many of our unique marine species are under threat from unsustainable commercial fishing, harmed or killed as bycatch. Much of our sea life is still recovering from centuries of hunting for the global fur, meat and oil trades. Today, numerous species of seabirds, turtles, sharks and marine mammals are legally recognised as threatened – their future is at risk. If you and I don't protect them, who will?

For over half a century, the Australian Marine Conservation Society has been on the front line fighting for a healthier future for the marine life that surrounds our island home – those wonderful sea animals that intrigue us, delight us, uplift and inspire us.

We are a leading voice for Australia's ocean wildlife, staffed by a committed group of professional and passionate scientists, educators, advocates and volunteers around the country who defend our precious oceans.

Our mission is to tackle the big issues facing the sea. We create marine sanctuaries, combat plastic pollution, make our fisheries sustainable, and protect and recover our endangered ocean wildlife, from the coastline out to the deep blue sea.

We also work to stop and reverse global ocean warming – certainly the biggest threat to our seas, and most notably our Great Barrier Reef. Global warming causes marine heatwaves, which in turn cause coral bleaching. Through the Fight for our Reef campaign we work to speed up Australia's transition from dirty fossil fuels that drive ocean warming to secure, clean energy at the scale and urgency required to keep life safe here on our beautiful blue planet.

Despite the enormous ongoing threats to our marine life, we have a long, proud history of defending their ocean homes.

Since the 1960s, we've been running a rolling campaign to protect Australia's Great Barrier Reef. We led Australia's largest sea-based campaign, which culminated in the declaration of the Great Barrier Reef Marine Park World Heritage Area – one of the most beautiful natural wonders on our planet.

We played a key role in the public campaign to ban commercial whaling in Australia, with the last whaling station closing in Albany in 1978. Since then we've been part of the push to free our southern oceans from harpoons, which we achieved in 2019.

Working with communities around Australia, we've secured bans on shark finning, moratoriums on seabed mining and, together with our patron Tim Winton, protection for Western Australia's Ningaloo Reef (think whale sharks, manta rays and fringing coral reefs).

We've also achieved habitat protection for critically endangered grey nurse sharks in New South Wales and Queensland, as well as protection from gillnet fisheries for sea lions in Western Australia.

We're proud of our role in achieving the world's largest marine parks network. Special parts of our Australian oceans are now protected across sixty large marine parks, including the Coral Sea, Ningaloo, Lord Howe and the Kimberley, as well as deep undersea mountains off Tasmania, where hundred-year-old fishes swim and ancient corals grow.

Our single proudest achievement, however, is having the support and trust of over 250,000 members of the Australian community. As a conservation charity, our work is made possible by passionate ocean lovers from coast to coast.

A journey of a thousand miles begins with a single step, and we hope that with this book you'll join us on a journey towards a healthier blue planet.

—Darren Kindleysides, CEO, Australian Marine Conservation Society

Earth

Patrick Tomkins

Ceridwen Dovey

Animal epiphanies

During the catastrophic January 2020 fires that burned half of Kangaroo Island, the story began to circulate that the local wildlife park had become the impromptu epicentre for the emergency treatment of burned wildlife. The place was soon inundated.

The park is owned by Dana and Sam Mitchell, a young couple who moved to the island in 2013, after they met working at a wildlife park in Victoria. They had already endured the stress of having to evacuate twice during the peak of the fires (the park was spared due to a last-minute change in wind direction), and initially found themselves unprepared for the new role thrust upon them.

Since the start of January, 650 koalas had been brought to their park by people unsure where else to take burned or injured animals. At first it was army personnel, State Emergency Services and firemen bringing in wildlife, but as the roads reopened, locals, too, began to bring in kangaroos and wallabies with their feet and paws melted off, who needed to be put out of their suffering. Orphaned koala joeys with burned ears or noses. Severely dehydrated older koalas with kidney issues. Possums blinded by the heat.

'We were having to make it up on the spot,' Sam told me. 'We were just a small wildlife park. These animals weren't my responsibility, but nobody else was doing anything, the government wasn't giving any direction.' In the first weeks, they operated the triage centre out of a tin shed, with no power.

David Maurice Smith

Sam and Dana soldiered on, and within three months established an impressive set-up for koala rescue, rehabilitation and release on the grounds of the park, beside the enclosures for the other 700 animals who live there (including snakes, cassowaries and a crocodile). New koala enclosures have been built behind their house, tended to by a dedicated group of vets and vet nurses from Australia Zoo, Zoos South Australia, and SAVEM (a veterinary equivalent of Doctors Without Borders). Trusted local volunteers have also put in the time and work to earn the respect of those in charge.

When I visited the koala clinic in early March, about two months after the fires, I found Dana in the middle of a complicated process of individually bottle-feeding around fifteen baby koalas, while also caring for her and Sam's little boy, Connor. The toddler was playing with the family dog, who is remarkably tolerant of both baby humans and a tiny kangaroo named Kylo, who practises its boxing on the dog's face.

Kirsten Latham, head koala keeper at Australia Zoo, was also doing individual baby koala feeds, and other staff and volunteers swirled in and out of the clinic, eating breakfast, or getting medical supplies. Dozens of slightly older rescued joey koalas (under eighteen months), who no longer depend on milk, are kept in enclosures outside, together with around thirty older rescued koalas – with names like Ralph, Bone Crusher and Pearl – though this number changes constantly, as those healthy enough to survive in the wild are released.

Dana was sitting on the sofa cradling an as-yet-unnamed baby koala in her arms, feeding it

David Maurice Smith

David Maurice Smith

At first, the ground was still smoking, and they had to wear special boots so the soles didn't melt. Now, the risk is of falling trees.

a morning bottle of Wombaroo (a lactose-free formula). 'She had no burns when we found her,' she said, 'but also no mum.' Kirsten had ten-month-old Duke swaddled in a towel. He was rescued in January with second-degree burns and no claws, and in the early days had to be force-fed with a syringe. Recently, he started taking the bottle. 'It helps to wrap them in a towel and keep a hand over their head and eyes,' she said. 'When they're drinking from their mums they keep their heads tucked right into the pouch, where it's dark and quiet.'

In the clinic's kitchen, Kailas Wild and Freya Harvey, both fit and sunburned, were studying the map of the island's blue-gum plantations on the wall, planning their next set of koala rescues. They are old friends, environmental activists and skilled climbers who have been on the island for weeks, doing the dangerous work of climbing the tall, burned trees to coax down koalas, which are often perched right at the very top.

Kailas and Freya have been working with a local ground rescue crew – Lisa and Jared Karran and their children, Saskia (fifteen) and Utah (thirteen). The Karrans live near Kingscote, where Jared is a policeman. They've spent almost every day since the fires out in the bush doing animal rescues. At first, the ground was still smoking, and they had to wear special boots so the soles didn't melt. Now, the risk is of falling trees. For up to twelve hours per day, they'll be out there, gloves and hard hats on, the kids uncomplaining. At last count, they've helped rescue 143 koalas.

'We were calling it Pompeii,' Lisa said, as we passed a tragic tableau of carbonised tammar wallabies huddled in a clearing beside burned blue gums.

Among the rows of charred trunks, Utah was getting an extendable koala pole ready, with a shredded feed bag attached to the end, which the climbers shake above the koala's head to scare it down the tree. Saskia had the cage ready at one of the tree bases. Jared had spotted this particular koala – 'because I'm koalified!' he joked – curled up right at the top of a black trunk devoid of leaves.

Recently the group rented a mechanised crane, which makes it easier to get to the tops of the trees, but there are still many rescues where the koala is so high up that Freya or Kailas need to clip in and use a throw-line to climb the precariously brittle trees, while shaking the koala pole above the animal's head.

The koalas grunt and squeal or bellow as they become aware of the disturbance, and can climb down the trunks amazingly fast. Once they've been plucked off at the bottom by Lisa or Utah, and are safely in the portable cage, they become surprisingly docile, gazing up at the humans peering in at them. The first koala rescued that day was underweight, and others had pink patches on their feet signalling previous (healed) burns, but many were healthy enough to be released elsewhere without needing to be checked by the vets at the Kangaroo Island Wildlife Park.

Hours passed like this in the hot plantations, yet the intensity of the group's work remained at a high pitch. It was gripping to watch. Each koala rescue had a unique emotional texture, a dramatic arc of growing tension as those on the ground waited for the climbers to encourage the koalas down the trunk, the adrenaline spike of grabbing them behind their strong necks and getting them into the transportation cage, the communal relief if they were found to be healthy.

For a while, the boundary between a person and animal is blurred and almost disappears. This can produce a flurry of intense emotions such as exaltation, confusion, wonder, and melancholy.

These rescues feel like a humane religion to cling to, in order not to descend into despair. Each one becomes a small but holy, tangible act taken to stem the wider suffering. It made me think of Roberto Marchesini's concept of 'animal epiphany', so beautifully described by animal historian Boria Sax in his forthcoming book, *Avian Illuminations*:

> For a while, the boundary between a person and animal is blurred and almost disappears. This can produce a flurry of intense emotions such as exaltation, confusion, wonder, and melancholy. Through an animal, a person achieves a renewed sense of what he is, yet also what he is not. Personal identity is challenged, redefined and expanded, yet ultimately reaffirmed.

That day, Kailas made his hundredth koala rescue. It also happened to be Jared's last day of doing rescues with his family; he'd used up all his annual leave. The next Monday, he would be back at work as a policeman. 'There'll be criminals robbing the bank, and I'll be totally distracted, gazing up into the trees still looking for koalas,' he said wistfully.

At dusk, the Karrans drove out to one of the only blue-gum plantations that didn't burn. They had six healthy koalas in the trunk of their car, rescued from plantations with no leaf cover for food. After the eerie silence of another long day spent in the burned plantations – not a single insect hum or bird song – it was a joy to see a flash of pink from the belly of a rose-breasted cockatoo, and to hear the soft, wave-like rustling of living eucalyptus leaves in the breeze. It felt like a patch of paradise that had not yet been lost.

Utah and Saskia released the koalas from the cages one by one, and the family laughed together as one of their feistiest rescues, a female koala with lovely fluffy ears, sprinted for a tree, climbed about five metres up, then stopped and stared back down at the humans for a good long while. Then she climbed higher, cosily wedged herself in the fork of a branch, and held on tightly as the narrow trunk rocked in the wind. *For a while, the boundary between a person and animal is blurred and almost disappears.*

10

This is an edited version of a longer article published in the June 2020 issue of the Smithsonian Magazine.

Ceridwen Dovey is a novelist and essayist. Her books include *Blood Kin, Only the Animals, In the Garden of the Fugitives* and *On J. M. Coetzee: Writers on writers*, and her most recent novel is *Life After Truth*. She writes for newyorker.com, *The Monthly* and the *Smithsonian Magazine*, and her work has been selected for *The Best Australian Science Writing 2020* and *2019*.

Dan Harley

Following a small possum into the dark

In 1994, I started following a small possum into the dark. Twenty-five years later I am still following. These possums have led me to places few venture – rainforest gullies with the echoes of dinosaurs, the quietness (and loneliness) of subalpine plateaus.

The story of Leadbeater's possum is a story about trees. And a story about fire. But also, a tale of the elusiveness of this animal. Most of the possum's history is veiled by the dense mists of the forests it inhabits. Cryptic and enigmatic, it disappeared entirely from view from 1910 to 1960, and was feared extinct.

The possum is endemic to Victoria, and totally different to the garden-variety possums that share our suburbs. In the 1970s some researchers suggested we rename these tiny, fast-moving sprites the fairy possum. Emerging at twilight, deep within ancient green forests, they would not be out of place in Tolkien's Middle Earth.

Now confined to seventy by ninety-five kilometres of forest on Melbourne's doorstep, the possum is already a victim of past climate change. All of its range is fire-prone. It is this restricted distribution that is the possum's greatest vulnerability.

Over this small geographical range, the possum inhabits three forest types, each of which has a different character, as do the possums that live there. Height is the challenge in the mountain ash forests – at night the forests are

Tim Bawden

intimidating simply because we are so dwarfed by the towering trees. Freezing temperatures are the challenge in the remote snow gum woodlands. Yet each night these small possums run into the white of winter. The lowland possums at Yellingbo are the last echo of the 'Great Swamp' that once stretched across the Koo-wee-rup district. Yellingbo is intimate, the possums are lower down. And the challenge to those who study the possums is water.

Much of my work with Leadbeater's possum has focused on the last swamp possums at Yellingbo, which are genetically distinct from their mountain counterparts. In the mid-1990s I started following the fate of each possum family there. A quarter of a century later, I continue to do so. I've held more of these possums in my hands than anyone in history, which feels like holding an amazing secret. Like us, they live in small family groups and are bound to particular places. For four years their forest home became my habitat. I would go to bed when they went to bed, camp next to their den trees. I lived the change of seasons with them. And no-one was watching. It was just me and them.

14

Over time I have seen the forest change. Dieback of vegetation has caused the number of possum families to plummet. Today, fewer than forty individual lowland possums remain. Without drastic intervention they will be lost.

Extinction is often described as an event when the last individual dies. In reality it is a process, as populations are diminished bit by bit.

Success ultimately equates to the number of possums. But how to succeed is with love.

In 2003, after a decade in the swamps of Yellingbo, I needed some sky and started searching for Leadbeater's possums in the subalpine zone. By 2007, we had established that they were widespread amid the snow gums of Lake Mountain.

As this realisation was sinking in, the Black Saturday fires struck in February 2009. The entire Lake Mountain plateau was severely burned. Barely a snow gum spared. All that remained of a Leadbeater's possum population that was several hundred strong pre-fire were five possums sheltering in one partly burned gully.

The soul left this place for a time. This patch of forest will not look the same in my lifetime. Lake Mountain was burned in the Black Friday wildfire of 1939 – I had forgotten the lesson that it could burn again.

The possums have shaped what I see, where I look when I search the horizon. They have been my rudder, and the lens through which I have explored. They live in places that are not comfortable for humans – they've prompted me to remove my insulation against the weather, to feel how it is shaping the land and its inhabitants. I have come to crave the feeling of winter.

It was these possums who introduced me to night in the forest. They've shown me nights when the moonlight is so strong you can walk without lights. Night in the forest provides time for reflection. Following the possum has taught me to look inwards.

I've been walking the same paths for over twenty years. Long enough to watch the trees change, hollows close over, homes that only the possums and I remember. And so this possum has given me a sense of place – a connection with country. Places I have spent time with my father. Places I will spend time with my children.

It was these possums who introduced me to night in the forest. They've shown me nights when the moonlight is so strong you can walk without lights. Night in the forest provides time for reflection. Following the possum has taught me to look inwards.

Leadbeater's possum has a knack of drawing people to it. In this respect, I am one among many. The possum has determined where I live, is weaved through the stories I tell my children, has shaped their imaginings, their drawings. It is part of my history, and I am part of its history.

15

Leadbeater's possum has survived ice ages. For millennia it has been poised in a delicate balance with fire. A balance we have disrupted. The possum challenges how we think about time. Tree hollows suitable for a family of possums take almost two centuries to develop. And fire can destroy them overnight.

All of our work to save Leadbeater's possum is underpinned by the importance of place. What happens to the land will ultimately determine what happens to this animal. Forest condition is key – how we manage fire and logging. An abundance of old growth is essential, yet it is something we have already lost.

We know what to do to save Leadbeater's possum. The science is strong. It is about making the choice to save it.

Prior to 1961, we thought we had lost the possum forever. It is rare to have a second chance to save a species, but that is what lies before us. History tells us one thing about this animal – take nothing for granted. Black Saturday was a crushing reminder of how quickly circumstances can change.

Every night I still head outside and stare into the inky blackness above and wonder about them. They still feel ethereal, near mythical. It is at this point that I feel most connected to the cosmos – in the quiet of night. I owe this gift to the possums.

Dan Harley investigated the ecology of the last lowland population of Leadbeater's possum as part of his PhD research. He continues to monitor this and other populations of the species. He has worked on recovery programs for a diverse range of threatened fauna across south-eastern Australia. In 2010, he joined Zoos Victoria, where his role involves developing and implementing recovery strategies for critically endangered species. He lives with his family in Healesville, with a view of Leadbeater's habitat.

Euan Ritchie

Dingo tales

It's a warm, humid night with a sky full of a seemingly impossible number of stars. The four of us are walking along a dry creek bed in a remote area of the Cape York Peninsula, in tropical North Queensland. By day we're here to revisit some of my old PhD study sites and survey antilopine wallaroo populations, but tonight we're doing what all good ecologists and nature lovers do: we're going spotlighting.

After seeing some of the usual suspects – tawny frogmouths, spotted nightjars and rather large and brilliantly green tree frogs – our attention is piqued by movement up ahead. We focus our torches on our night-time companion and instantly recognise its identity: a dingo. We walk towards it, *carefully* – after all, my wife and I have our two kids, aged four and seven, in tow. But the dingo is well and truly aware of our presence too, and effortlessly jumps up and over the creek bank in a few bounds, slipping away into the darkness. The brief but magical encounter has ended, or so we think.

What we discover next is something we'll cherish forever. As we continue walking along the creek bed, past the area where the dingo disappeared, I see movement again, but this time at the base of a large dead gum tree, where there's an entrance big enough for a wombat to pass through gracefully (if wombats lived in Cape York, that is). I walk over and investigate the hollow, and realise two things: the dingo we saw is a female, and she was executing a cunning plan, trying to draw us away from the tree.

Angus Emmott

Neatly tucked inside it are her three pups. As we get closer for a better look, the pups retreat further into the base of the tree. They are timid; perhaps it's the first time they've seen humans. We take a quick look, a passable photo on my phone, and leave them in peace. No doubt Mum will return to the den and reassure them soon.

Some label dingoes vicious, dangerous killers, but it's hard to accept these sentiments when staring into their eyes. Our experience highlighted to us how misunderstood and awfully mistreated these animals are.

My relationship with one of Australia's most enigmatic and polarising species blossomed in 2008. That was the year I began research with colleagues at James Cook University into dingo ecology, management and conservation. More than a decade later, I continue to work on and attempt to understand this species. Dingoes have taught me a lot: about the important roles of large predators – about how, for example, keeping kangaroo and feral goat numbers in check can benefit plants and other animals. But they have also taught me just as much about people, underscoring our ongoing unhealthy relationship with this ancient land following the European invasion roughly 230 years ago.

I met my very first *wild* dingo in 1996. It helped me mark and forever remember another key moment in my life: moving from Melbourne to Townsville to begin university study. Returning from an evening out with new friends on one of my first nights in Townsville, I found a dingo lying nonchalantly near the front door of the university gatehouse.

Perhaps it was a momentary glimpse of the closer bond I would develop with this fascinating and undeniably beautiful species. It helped to affirm that I was in the right place, despite being more than 2500 kilometres from home, family and friends. I'm so grateful for that opportunity to study in Queensland because I can't imagine being anything but what I am now – a wildlife ecologist with a deep commitment to conserving our remarkable fauna.

Not all dingoes can afford to be as relaxed as the one I saw that night. There's no question dingoes can cause severe problems. Sheep torn asunder not only affect the profitability of some grazing enterprises but, worse still, can lead to awful stress and devastating mental-health outcomes for livestock producers. As a

We simply haven't moved past our brutal colonial ways and learnt to live more in tune with this country and its inhabitants.

Angus Emmott

Angus Emmott

result, we are at war with dingoes in some regions of Australia.

I don't use the word *war* lightly. Consider these facts: Australia built the world's longest fence, the approximately 5500-kilometre dingo barrier fence, to keep them out of prime livestock grazing country. In some rural areas, scores of lifeless dingoes swing in the wind, hanging from trees. And millions of dollars are also spent annually on deploying poison baits for dingoes.

All of this saddens and deeply troubles me, because it's our failure writ large. We simply haven't moved past our brutal colonial ways and learnt to live more in tune with this country and its inhabitants. We *can* protect dingoes, livestock and livelihoods, and science teaches us that non-lethal approaches, such as using guardian dogs (think Oddball), offer great promise in this respect. We just need to be more open to doing things differently.

One last Cape York dingo tale. It's my wife's birthday and we're doing a pre-dawn wallaroo survey at Piccaninny Plains, one of Australian Wildlife Conservancy's sanctuaries. As our 4WD slowly rattles and weaves along a dusty, dry track, the sun begins to cast its soft morning light, illuminating my favourite habitat: tropical savanna woodland. As we round a corner, we come across a young dingo. We quickly pull out the camera, thinking that this might be another brief encounter. But we're wrong.

The dingo quietly and calmly trots alongside us for several minutes, staying about a hundred metres or so from our vehicle. It's clearly relaxed and unperturbed, and we are equally curious about each other. For me it's another reminder that, as with our relationships with sharks, crocodiles and other predators, nothing is black or white, and we must find better solutions to human–wildlife conflict.

I've been lucky enough to hear the primal howl of dingoes carrying over the sand dunes of Victoria's Big Desert Wilderness region by night, and I wish more people might experience such a rare privilege. Connecting with these animals, and others, is what it means to be alive.

Dr Euan Ritchie is a father of two and Associate Professor in Wildlife Ecology and Conservation at Deakin University. Euan has spent much of his career so far studying animals such as antilopine wallaroos, dingoes, frogs, tree kangaroos, red foxes and feral cats, to help inform pest management and the conservation of native wildlife. He also spends considerable time teaching, and communicating his research with the public, inspiring many others about the wonders of nature and the urgent need to care for it.

Emma Viskic

Phascogales: A love story

I first saw the sanctuary on a crisp autumn day, a grey landscape of fallen timber and coppiced ironbark trees. It's Dja Dja Wurrung country, dry and fragile. The ground is rocky, veined with the iron-ringed remains of the old wooden pipes that once carried water to nearby Castlemaine.

It took a day for me to fall for the place, years to recognise its subtle seasons. The area was almost destroyed by postcolonial grazing and felling, but is now a haven for both humans and animals; two hundred acres of covenanted land.

It was here that I first saw a brush-tailed phascogale, a nocturnal marsupial so shy and glamorous that I initially thought it was a figment of my imagination. Its large ears and narrow nose appeared from the crook of an ironbark tree, then a tiny grey body, followed by an outrageous, feathery tail. We stared at each other in surprise, then it scampered down the trunk, swishing its tail like a grande dame flicking a feather boa. And I was in love.

Phascogales only live for a few years. The females, that is. The males live for twelve months, dying after a short period of frenzied mating. Threatened by cats and foxes, the increasing loss of their natural habitat – ironbark forests – makes them even more vulnerable.

The importance of saving the phascogale's habitat was one of the reasons the sanctuary was established in the 1970s. It was founded by a group of writers, actors and artists who pooled their meagre savings to buy and save

William Terry

the land. They've cared for it ever since.

I was lucky enough to join the collective a decade ago, and have a tiny one-room shack where I escape to write. A few times a year, we gather to trade stories and tend the land. We thin the overgrown ironbark to leave room for undergrowth, install boxes for the phascogales and sugar gliders, plant seedlings and build deer-proof fences. Tiny native orchids and yellow-headed myrrnong have returned to the rocky ground, and the scars from the water pipes fill with moss in winter. Flocks of mournful currawongs live here now, along with echidnas and black-nosed wallabies.

The phascogales are thriving. They share the land graciously with the rest of us, venturing from the trees at night with a flourish of their tails, then quickly vanish into the darkness.

Emma Viskic is the author of the Caleb Zelic series: *Resurrection Bay* (winner of the Ned Kelly Award for Best First Fiction, and three Davitt Awards), *And Fire Came Down* (winner of the Davitt Award for Best Novel) and *Darkness For Light*.

25

William Terry

Clare Wright

Possum magic: A curly tale

With thanks to Mem Fox and Alison Lester

At our beach, our magic beach, there are a couple of days every summer that my family calls 'bushfire days'. These are the days that start warm and still, when you want to be in the waves early. You know that before long it will be too hot to cross the dunes to the ocean, and sure enough, by mid-morning the wind has come up and by lunchtime you're battling a howling north-westerly. It comes hollering across the paddocks, belting down the beach, whipping up sand and fury. The air is desiccating and the sea provides no respite. On bushfire days, the only place to be is indoors. Sweltering, suffocating, waiting it out until 'the change' inevitably arrives.

We have another family vernacular for these intermittent summer scorchers: possums-dropping-out-of-trees days.

Because they do. There's no smoke, no flame, but it is so oppressively hot that the possums literally fall from the tinder-dry melaleucas. You find them the next day, after the change has come, at the feet of trees, under powerlines, stiff.

On one such day a few summers back, my sister and I couldn't bear lying about in our fibro shack any longer. We were sweaty, crotchety and not so much bored as too lethargic to read, too limp to play cards, too damned hot to sleep. So we drenched our sarongs in cold water, wrapped them around our bathers, and went for a walk down a tea-tree-lined bush track.

Kristian Bell

Tucked behind the dunes, we were shielded from the north-westerly. The heat was savage, but the languid movement felt good. We dipped in and out of conversation. It was eerily quiet. The birds must have been conserving their energy too.

We almost didn't see her. Ambling along, mesmerised, Miranda-like. It was my sister who spotted the puffball of tawny fur sitting by the side of the track. We stopped, expecting whatever creature it was to scamper on our approach. But she didn't move, just sat there, staring blankly at the ground, glassy eyed, dazed.

I pulled my still-damp sarong from my shoulders and, arms outstretched, crept slowly towards what it became clear was a fat ringtail possum. Crouched before her now, she still didn't move. But she blinked. Rigid – with what? Fear? Pain? – but not stiff. She made no attempt to bolt as I swept her up in my sarong and pulled her to my chest.

Over the years we've found many orphaned possum babies. The local wildlife shelter – which in this case is a lovely old lady in the next town over with a lounge room full of eagles, koalas and blue-tongue lizards – had taught me what to do. Pop the wee babe in a sock and tuck her in your bra. Left boob. Carry her around during the day and sleep her on a lukewarm hot water bottle placed at the bottom of a washing basket at night. Feed her drops of sugar water. Bring her to me if you're worried.

But what to do with a full-grown possum? On a 42-degree day? And one, I could now detect, as I carefully peeled back my sarong to take a peek, who had two little hind legs poking out of her soft pouch. No, wait, make that four little legs, and two tiny curled, white-tipped tails. No wonder this possum was stunned. The jill had fallen out of her tree, carrying two joeys with her.

Back at the shack, I opted for a version of the wildlife lady's counsel. In our bedroom, we have one of those ubiquitous Ikea shelving units, beloved of beach houses, children's playrooms and yoga studios alike. Five by five square compartments. Some squares open, housing books, rolled towels, jars of jam and preserves; others holding matching baskets in an array of tasteful Scandinavian colours. It was into one of these storage cubes, upended of its socks and undies, that I carefully placed the possum,

We almost didn't see her. Ambling along, mesmerised, Miranda-like. It was my sister who spotted the puffball of tawny fur sitting by the side of the track.

her babies, the sarong, a little bowl of sugar water, and some tea-tree twigs that my daughter snapped off 'to make her feel at home'. This whole unlikely ecosystem I then slid back into place, just one of twenty-five squares of summer living. Dark. Breathable. Safe.

And here Jill lived for the following week. The change came, and with it, rain. The temperature dropped twenty degrees in as many minutes. Jill began to move around in her box. I could hear her scratching about at night. The chunks of apple and banana my daughter lovingly fed through the top of the box were gone by morning. I topped up her water. Furry little feet darted in and out of the soft mound of Jill's pouch. Every so often – not *too* often, I'd tell the kids, and the other kids they brought around to see 'our' possum – we'd pull the box out of its square space and give Jill a little pat. She looked up at us with beady black eyes, never flinching at the touch or attempting to scarper out of the box, though she clearly now had the strength and energy to do so.

Over the years we've found many orphaned possum babies. The local wildlife shelter – which in this case is a lovely old lady in the next town over with a lounge room full of eagles, koalas and blue-tongue lizards – had taught me what to do.

One night, I decided this was the moment to return Jill to the bush. There was nothing in particular that guided my judgement, just a hasty but abiding sense that it was *time*. The evening air was still and mild, the clear sky dotted by a trillion southern stars. If I was to be liberated, I would want my captivity to end on such a night as this.

I carried Jill, enfolded in her now stinky sarong, to the end of our street and a few metres into the tea-tree scrub, daughter trailing behind, designated torchbearer. Stopping next to a solid banksia, I unwrapped our precious parcel and reached out to place Jill on a branch just above eye level. There she sat, calmly staring at me. 'Go sweet thing,' I cooed at her, 'you're well now. Go.'

But Jill did not go. She just sat there looking at me. Not listless. Just motionless.

'What's wrong with her?' my daughter asked.

'I'm not sure,' I answered, truthfully. 'Maybe she's not ready to go back.'

I reached out to give Jill a little tap on her rump – go on, shoo – and that's when she climbed onto my hand and scampered back up my arm, coming to rest on my shoulder. Her ringtail curled up in my collarbone. I carried her back to the house and returned our guest to her quarters.

Two nights later, we had friends over for dinner. Barbecue, deck, beers. The possum story was told.

'So she's still here,' said Johnny. 'Can I have a look?'

Johnny sat on the edge of our bed as I slipped Jill's box out from its cubbyhole. Now confident that I could handle her, I picked Jill up and placed her on the bed. Johnny, an athletic brick of a man with sun-bleached blond hair and a no-frills approach to life, lay back on his side, gazing at Jill, entranced.

'Isn't she beautiful?' I purred. Just as Johnny was about to answer, Jill started moving. She crept forward a few paces, then started rocking back and forth, scraping her belly on the doona. After a few more rhythmic lunges, Jill expelled the contents of her pouch onto the bed. She stepped away, turned to look at the soft mass she'd left behind, then crawled back into her box.

Not a foot away from Johnny's ice-blue eyes lay the fetid, tangled mass of two dead joeys, each no bigger than my thumb, their exquisite ringtails entwined.

Johnny let out a strange, strangled gulp, like he was trying hard to muffle a lifetime of pain. A single fat tear rolled down his cheek and seeped into the doona.

He came with me and my daughter when we took Jill back out to the scrub that night. Again, I lifted her onto the banksia branch. Again, she sat impassively, staring at me. But then she crooked her furry fawn neck and looked towards the trunk of the tree, towards the dark tangle of foreshore scrub that lay beyond. Jill turned one last time to cast her shiny black eyes upon me. And then she was gone.

Yesterday I walked the track behind the dunes again. This time, in early May, I was sheltering from the prevailing south-westerly. The radio warned of storm-force winds, and there was no way I was going to brave the wild and woolly beach. Not even the dogs wanted to cross the dunes. Swaddled

She crooked her furry fawn neck and looked towards the trunk of the tree, towards the dark tangle of foreshore scrub that lay beyond. Jill turned one last time to cast her shiny black eyes upon me. And then she was gone.

in a beanie, scarf and thermals, dogs darting in and out of ferny undergrowth dripping from the overnight rain, I counted seven types of mushroom along the path. Slimy rust-coloured bells. Flat white orbs with scalloped edges that looked more like sea creatures than fungi. Creamy buttons in perfect fairy rings.

And I wondered, where do the possums go to weather the circle of life, insistent, pervasive, unyielding?

Professor Clare Wright OAM is an award-winning historian, author, broadcaster and public commentator. She is currently a Principal Research Fellow and ARC Future Fellow at La Trobe University. In 2020, Clare was awarded a Medal of the Order of Australia in the Australia Day Honours List for 'services to literature and to historical research'. She is the author of four works of history, including the bestselling *The Forgotten Rebels of Eureka* (winner of the Stella Prize) and *You Daughters of Freedom*.

Marissa Parrott

For the love of the Devil,
and its devilish little cousins

Anyone who thinks Tasmanian devils are the most fearsome animal in
Australia has never met their tiny dasyurid – carnivorous marsupial –
cousins. The first time I met a dasyurid, it promptly sunk its teeth through
the top of my fingernail into the sensitive nail bed and drew blood. To add
insult to injury, it had just eaten a member of the species I was studying –
the world's smallest gliding mammal, the feathertail glider – in its nest. This
voracious hunter – a tiny 25-gram agile antechinus – had a big personality,
but was only the size of my thumb.

I was intrigued by its fighting spirit and impressive hunting abilities – so
much so that when I started my PhD the following year, it was on the love life
of the agile antechinus.

This species, a smaller relative of the more famous Tasmanian devil, has
a remarkable life strategy. It has a highly synchronised two-week annual
breeding season in winter; the females mate with up to seven different males
and store their sperm to ensure they have a healthy litter of babies. Females
can then give birth to litters with multiple fathers – each litter of up to ten
young can have as many as five fathers, so those born together are actually
half-siblings.

Meanwhile, the males mate with everyone they can find, fight among
themselves, forget to eat and, after two weeks, all drop dead from stress. They
die within a few days of each other, leaving the females to raise their babies in

Marissa Parrott

Marissa Parrott

a population completely devoid of adult males.

During my research, I found that females choose males that are genetically different to themselves, based on their smell, and that those males have the highest siring success in the litter. This finding led to my career of using mate selection to help endangered species breeding programs.

The next species I worked with during my postdoctoral research was another delightful dasyurid – the stripe-faced dunnart. Like the antechinus, this tiny predator has an amazing breeding strategy. It has the shortest pregnancy of any known mammal. Stripe-faced dunnarts are pregnant for just eleven days. And they give birth to babies smaller than Tic Tacs. Much smarter than us!

Over the coming years I would be fortunate to work with a variety of voracious, clever and beautiful dasyurids: the fluffy-tailed desert-dwelling kultarr, the nimble woodland-dwelling red-tailed phascogale, and the feisty rock-running Ningbing false antechinus, as well as multiple species of dunnarts, antechinus, and magnificently spotted quolls. It was only a matter of time before I met and fell in love with the biggest dasyurid of them all: the Tasmanian devil.

Devils are a very sweet, shy and lovely species, with a bad (and largely unfounded) reputation. They have a striking and eerie voice, almost a scream. When European settlers first heard Devils calling in the night, they said the only thing that could make such a noise was a devil. When Devils are stressed, their little ears go red (a bit like devil horns) – so you have the makings of a devilish name.

I have been lucky to work with Devils for over

The animals I know are clever, cheeky, shy and make wonderful mums. The photos you usually see have them looking aggressive – mouths open wide, showing their huge teeth. But this actually isn't a sign of an angry Devil. They often yawn when they are uncertain or worried and they want to avoid conflict by looking big and tough.

twelve years at Zoos Victoria, and the animals I know are clever, cheeky, shy and make wonderful mums. The photos you usually see have them looking aggressive – mouths open wide, showing their huge teeth. But this actually isn't a sign of an angry Devil. They often yawn when they are uncertain or worried and want to avoid conflict by looking big and tough.

Despite their often gentle nature, they are very resilient creatures. Devils can live in areas that reach 40 degrees Celsius in summer, then through freezing, snowy winters. They often carry scars of conflicts over food or mates, and traverse amazingly remote and rugged landscapes. They can travel over twenty kilometres per night.

Devils can bite straight through bone. They have the strongest bite force (relative to body weight) of any mammal – and remarkably big jaw muscles, which give them their round teddy-bear-like faces. Their strong teeth and jaws are put to good use. They can eat up to 40 per cent of their own body weight in one sitting and then don't need to eat again for days.

Females give birth to around thirty tiny babies (each about the size of a grain of rice), but have only four teats in their pouch, so only four of the young can attach to a teat and grow – survival of the fittest from birth.

Tasmanian devil joeys may be the cutest babies in the animal kingdom, with their fuzzy black fur, bright little eyes and gummy grins. They are playful, bouncing balls of fun as they learn to hunt, socialise and become functional members of Devil society. Devils are generally a solitary species and prefer to live alone. However, they meet at communal latrine sites to deposit their scents, and at carcasses, where they work in a group to pull apart their food. They often then stay and eat together.

Baby Devils are good at climbing trees while they are wriggly and nimble, though they often lose this skill as they grow stockier, fill out their muscle and become less agile. I have had the pleasure of spending time with joeys being hand-raised after losing their mum – they like to chase feet, chew shoelaces and snuggle in for naps. But they retain their devilish natures – they are truly wild animals.

I have worked closely with the Devils in our conservation breeding program at Zoos Victoria's Healesville Sanctuary, with our partners in the Save the Tasmanian Devil Program, as well as in the wilds of Tasmania. Each Devil has its own personality and cheeky nature. There is Katniss, the wonderful mum at Healesville who carries her joeys on her back and ducks for them every time she walks into her den; Mulana, the orphaned Devil who loves climbing tree ferns and training with her keepers; and Usher, the clever wild Devil who outsmarted us all and learnt how to steal food from our traps without being caught. While it was frustrating that he thwarted our attempts to survey the population and ruined all our hard work, we had to admire his ingenuity!

Sadly, Devils are an endangered species. They suffer from a unique and horrifying form of transmissible cancer, devil facial tumour disease, which has killed an estimated 80 per cent of wild Devils so far, and they are hit by cars on our roads, adding to our loss. Everyone can help them by supporting their conservation programs and slowing down for wildlife when driving, especially at night.

I am one of hundreds of people who love Devils and work to fight extinction for this amazing species. We ensure that their unnervingly beautiful voices are still heard in the night, and that those gummy joey smiles are still seen. Devils are such an important species in their ecosystem, and in our hearts. I work every day to help save them, so others have the chance to fall for them, and their smaller cousins, just as I did – although preferably without a punctured fingernail.

38

Dr Marissa Parrott is the Reproductive Biologist for Zoos Victoria. She works across Healesville Sanctuary, Werribee Open Range Zoo, Melbourne Zoo and numerous field locations to improve reintroduction and captive breeding success, and lead reproductive and behavioural research, for some of the world's most endangered species. She is also involved in wildlife and conservation programs across Australia, Asia, Africa and the Americas. Marissa passionately supports Zoos Victoria's commitment that no Victorian terrestrial vertebrate species will ever go extinct.

Lucy Treloar

The valley of lizards

There's a place in South Australia that I know quite well – at least I thought I did – a shallow valley formed by a landslip along the bottom of a line of ancient hills. Hardly anyone goes there. Even on a windy day, it's the most peaceful place I know.

Different plants spring up there, sheltered by the lip of the valley: soursobs, freesias, pincushion flowers, wild oats that turn white-gold in summer, hardy bushes bearing small berries beloved by birds, and so on, the seasons and plants easing into each other. They're mostly outsiders there, like me.

An ancient pathway of red earth, hard and smooth, threads the valley's length, and on this spring day, as I was walking the path, it all felt utterly familiar, though I had never before visited at this exact time of year. A warm breeze was bending the grasses. High above, two kestrels sauntered the wind's pathways against the vaporous blue sky.

It might have been a chunk of dark wood ahead – odd, but I was walking fast and not thinking. I would likely have stepped over it or around it, or kicked it aside. But the thing moved and came alive, rotating slowly, like the dial of a compass. I paid attention then. One end of it flipped open – a shocking wide pink maw – and hissed. Then, quite slowly, with a sort of ponderous grace (if that was possible), it eased off the path and disappeared beneath a scrubby bush.

I was almost breathless. It was as if the natural world had run at me and

screamed in my face, 'Remember your place. You are nothing here, nothing!' And I knew it was right. Sometimes you see the world anew; the beloved familiar becomes alien. It was a lizard, but not one I'd ever seen. Around the small nearby village there were sizeable blue-tongues, but this was something else entirely: blackish, hefty, armoured, marbled in gold, with short little legs and a clubbed tail.

Here they'd been, these prehistoric things, one of the great slow heartbeats of an ancient world beating alongside ours.

There were more of them at distant intervals along the path, luxuriating on the baked earth the way my dogs do on brick paving. One or two moved about slowly, and I walked slowly too, trying not to alarm them. Everything about them was slow – apart from the startling mouth-flipping-open move.

I crouched near one, right down low, and looked about, trying to imagine their world: the grass and bushes turning to lush, light-filled forests on either side; the way the lizards rested there, oblivious to the ferocious ants. And once their blood had warmed, the way they promenaded down these avenues of dappled light in a ponderous *passeggiata* towards tender new growth, or perhaps a few flowers. I thought of vibrations beneath my feet, danger approaching, slow flight into the undergrowth and a cautious blinking reappearance into heat and light when it – I – had passed.

In this way I discovered that the world I had been ambling through for decades in a lordly way belonged to other beings entirely. Here they'd been, these prehistoric things, one of the great slow heartbeats of an ancient world beating alongside ours. They were living out their lives in as unchanged a way as people's actions allowed. And I was witnessing it. It was almost overwhelming. The words that come to mind – gratitude, joy, wonderment, elation – diminish rather than describe that moment. But there's nothing wrong with nature transcending words, is there?

I didn't even know what they were, but I found out with no trouble at all. They were a species of blue-tongue lizard, *Tiliqua rugosa*, that's also called garrbaali (Yuwaalaraay), manggaay (Gamilaraay), the bobtail goanna, or the shingleback, stumpy-tail, pinecone or sleepy lizard. It seems they live all across southern Australia, are heavily armoured – which, considering their speed, makes sense – and vary in colour from black through to cream, depending on their range. They live for fifty years in the wild; they have friends and enemies and complex social networks, visiting each other and sharing safe places overnight before finding their way home, like the slowest of homing pigeons. They're also monogamous (a characteristic unknown in other lizards), with couples staying close during spring and summer, and have been seen to grieve when a mate dies, hanging around for days, trying to nudge them back to life.

But let's not say they're like people, though we might recognise some common behaviours; let's say that they are themselves, and that their lives have value to them, and that on the basis of their highly evolved needs, habits, preferences and instincts they are not suited to the diminished life of solitary captivity that some people find it entertaining to observe. Thinking of these things, alongside my wonderment, I also felt fear. It was the thought of their vulnerability. And that's why I say, let them be.

That passing encounter happened only by chance. I might never have known of this other layer of life, another world quietly continuing alongside mine. I love thinking of the valley of lizards, of the lizards out sunning themselves, but I won't go back at that time of year. It's the easiest thing for one person's wonderment to turn into a destructive scrum. People are so thoughtlessly inquisitive. Think of the fairy penguins on Victoria's coastline and the industry that has become. The fact that we don't mean ill hardly matters.

Shingleback lizards have enough stressors. Habitat fragmentation is weakening their genetic diversity. More recently, studies into the effects of climate change on shinglebacks show a high sensitivity to water loss, alongside some adaptation to high temperatures, during which they retreat deep into burrows, emerging after heavy rainfall.

Reflecting on the careless destructiveness of people, American writer Annie Dillard says, 'It is difficult to undo our own damage, and to recall to our presence that which we have asked to leave.' People might not miss them if they weren't there, might hardly recall them after a while – though I think I would. I'll think of that perfect walk, the lizards ambling beneath the high blue sky, and let that be enough.

42

Lucy Treloar's latest novel, *Wolfe Island*, was shortlisted for the NSW Premier's Literary Award for Fiction and for the ABIA Literary Fiction Book of the Year. She is also the author of the novel *Salt Creek* (2015), which won the Indie Book Award for Best Debut, the ABIA Matt Richell Award and the Dobbie Literary Award, and was shortlisted for prizes including the Miles Franklin Literary Award and the UK's Walter Scott Prize.

Chris Flynn

'The bluey will thank you'

In 2019 I moved to Phillip Island (Bunurong name: Millowl), a spot best known for its motorcycle grand prix and penguin parade. The diversity and abundance of wildlife on the island is overwhelming. In addition to the 32,000 famous fairy penguins, there are koalas, humpback whales, orca, peregrine falcons, endangered hooded plovers, short-tailed shearwaters who commute annually between the island and Alaska, thousands of Cape Barren geese who poop all over the footy oval, copperhead snakes (only the seventh most venomous snake in the world, so nothing to worry about), 30,000 fur seals, and an introduced population of eastern barred bandicoots.

In short, the place is teeming with animal life.

While out for a walk last spring, with a hardened journalist friend from Melbourne, we encountered three snakes in twenty minutes (there may have been unseemly shrieking), dozens of swamp wallabies, countless birds and, right there in the middle of the trail, a blotched blue-tongue lizard.

This glorious creature is essentially a large skink, with adults measuring up to fifty centimetres. Its colourful tongue acts as a warning to predators, who think the lizard might be venomous. In fact, they are gentle souls who can live for up to thirty years.

When I mentioned the encounter to the president of the Phillip Island Motorcycle Club, Darryl Jones, his reply was unexpected: 'Did you remove her ticks?'

Matt Clancy

He explained that blue-tongues, or 'blueys', have a large head and prominent earholes, which they cannot reach with their stubby front legs. Ticks lodge in their ears and drive them crazy. When Darryl discovers a blue-tongue while out walking, he gently scoops the lizard up, checks its ears and removes any invasive ticks by pinching them out with his nails.

'The bluey will thank you,' he assures me.

He is not wrong. Ticks are horrible little bloodsucking parasites and the idea of having one in your ear doesn't bear thinking about.

The opportunity to carry out my civic lizard duty arose a few weeks later. I was out for a morning walk on Cape Woolamai, a nature reserve with stunning views of surf to the south and a tranquil bay to the north. I often swim there, at an abandoned granite quarry not far from 'Spew Hill' – a steep sand dune kids careen down on boogie boards.

The relaxed blue-tongue lizard felt like an alien creature. Her stubby feet scrabbled against my skin, so I quickly inspected her ears for parasites. Finding none, I set her down in the same spot as before. She acted as if nothing had happened.

After a dip in the chilly water, I was making my way back along the trail when I spotted a bluey lurking in the grass by the edge of the track. She made no attempt to flee, and so, as I had been instructed by Darryl, I got down on my knees and scooped her up in my palms. This was only the second time in my life I had touched reptilian scales, and it was a curious feeling. The relaxed blue-tongue lizard felt like an alien creature. Her stubby feet scrabbled against my skin, so I quickly inspected her ears for parasites. Finding none, I set her down in the same spot as before. She acted as if nothing had happened.

From her perspective, this was correct. From mine, however, a threshold had been crossed. A precedent had been set. I had entered the lizard kingdom, where I now proudly held the lowly rank of tick inspector.

Chris Flynn is the author of *Mammoth*, *The Glass Kingdom* and *A Tiger in Eden* (shortlisted for the Commonwealth Book Prize). His work has also appeared in the *Guardian*, the *Age*, the *Australian*, *Griffith Review*, *Meanjin* and many other publications.

David Lindenmayer

Essence of glider

Scientists are not supposed to be emotional people. Our training is to present facts – in as few words as possible and without feeling. Yet there is a photo in my office – now faded with age and too much sunlight – that never fails to stir my emotions.

It's of a youthful me; on one arm is my six-month-old son with a dummy in his mouth, and on the other is a heavily sedated greater glider wearing a newly fitted radio collar. The image embodies my two biggest passions – my family and Australian wildlife. It reminds me that conserving Australia's environment is important not only for our wildlife, but also for our children (and all children), so they can continue to experience the wonders of the natural world.

Most people won't have heard of the greater glider. You could think of it as a small gliding koala, in that its diet is almost exclusively eucalyptus leaves. And, as is the case with koalas, not just any kind of eucalypt will do. The greater glider typically selects trees with the most nutrient-rich leaves, growing in the most productive parts of the landscape.

Its small size (gliders weigh about 1.2 kilograms) is quite remarkable, given that most animals with a diet comprised solely of leaves are relatively large, such as the koala, which can weigh up to 15 kilograms. The greater glider is almost the smallest a mammal with its particular diet can be. Gliders have to eat large quantities to survive. But the glider's diet goes beyond survival – it

Caleb McElrea

influences the animal's breeding system too. Population densities are highest in the most productive forests, where there is typically one male glider for every two females and the mating system is polygamous. In less productive forests, population densities are lower and the sex ratio is one to one, making the animals monogamous. Whether they have one partner or two, gliders don't seem to care about fur colour. Some gliders are pure white, others are jet black with a white underbelly, and yet others are a mix of black, white and grey. I have seen many multicoloured pairs.

Gliders also don't commit to one home. They live in hollows in large old trees, but do not restrict themselves to just one hollow. They move from one to another, possibly as a way of avoiding being caught by predators. But while they have several homes, they are selective when it comes to nest sites, typically choosing the tallest tree they can find. There's a reason they need the extra height. Gliders don't fly. They 'volplane' away from the top of their nest trees, in a kind of daring dive, when they first emerge at dusk. Sometimes they cover distances of over a hundred metres in a single glide.

To make their domestic arrangements even more complicated, greater gliders don't like eating at home. They rarely feed in the same trees as they nest in, possibly to reduce the risk that predators will discover where they spend their daylight hours. Any animal wanting to make a meal of a glider will need sharp eyes, because their ears will be little use. Greater gliders are almost completely silent in the forest, making very few calls – although they sometimes give their presence away with the thud they make after completing a glide and landing in a tree.

I most often see greater gliders while doing dusk surveys in Victoria's mountain ash forests. At dusk, the animals emerge from a hollow high up in a huge living or dead tree, and sit, quietly grooming, before volplaning to a distant part of the forest. Several times I've witnessed the extraordinary sight of a glider zooming silently just over my head – so close that I could see the animal's gliding membranes rippling. Simply being there is magical – giant trees, supreme silence and amazing creatures. I have spent more than 1000 nights doing surveys for animals like the greater glider over many decades, and that unique experience of quietly observing nature in beautiful forest environments is always a deeply spiritual one.

The sound of a glider thudding into a tree is less common than it used to be. Their numbers are plummeting in Victoria, New South Wales and Queensland. These losses are occurring in some unexpected places such as large and well-protected national parks. It comes back to those all-important tall old trees. The gliders can't live without them, but populations of these trees are declining in the vast majority of Australia's forests and woodlands.

The gliders also die in wildfires. They are killed in logging operations. They cannot survive land clearing. They simply die in their trees and territories when a forest is logged – and it may be decades or even centuries before the population can recover – if they recover at all.

In many ways, they are a sentinel species, warning us when the disturbances caused by fire, logging and climate change have become truly overwhelming. They are very vulnerable to the high temperatures associated with Australia's rapidly warming climate.

Every day, I worry that the greater glider may become extinct. It is hard to comprehend that such a wonderful animal could be lost in my lifetime, especially when so many people have worked so hard and for so long to stop this from happening.

In the photograph of me, my son and the glider, I'm wearing a red velcro band threaded through an old diving watch. I have fond memories of that watchband – it was old and tatty, because whenever we caught gliders in the wild they would let go of a night's store of urine. My watch and hands would be covered in the stuff.

Glider urine is highly concentrated, derived from eucalyptus leaves, the animal's sole source of food. Perhaps only a biologist would admit that the powerful smell is not unpleasant!

They say that songs remind you of places and people. But I think smells can too. 'Essence of glider' reminded me of a special time in my life, with young kids, working in a wonderful forest with incredible animals, a time long gone, when gliders were easy to find and intact old forests were common. The watchband is gone, so is the watch. But I still have that photo. I hope it won't be the only thing left.

David Lindenmayer AO is Professor of Ecology and Conservation Biology at the Australian National University's Fenner School of Environment and Society. He has had forty-five books and more than 790 peer-reviewed papers published on a wide range of topics associated with forestry, woodlands, wildlife and biodiversity conservation, and ecologically sustainable natural resource management. He is the most cited forest ecologist in the world and his conservation and biodiversity research has been recognised through numerous awards, including the Eureka Science Prize (twice), the Whitley Award (eleven times) and the Australian Natural History Medallion.

Ella Loeffler

Under the shade of the eucalypts

I move to Australia when I am just a seedling, sprout my roots and form shiny green leaves. Oak trees and cyclamens replaced by flowering gums, I learn English reading *Possum Magic*, my foreign accent slowly melting as I read about Hush and Grandma Poss. I worry that Hush will stay invisible forever, vanish and never come back, and am relieved when his furry face reappears on the glossy pages, munching on his Vegemite sandwich.

Under the shade of eucalypts and acacias at my local park, I befriend the native ducks and magpies, magpie larks, rainbow lorikeets and herons. I feed them bread before I know I shouldn't, collect gumnuts, chase my dog, sing songs of fairies and possums.

As a sapling I study rainforests and deserts, marsupials and eucalypts. I learn that kangaroos can pause their pregnancy in times of drought, and that the oil in eucalyptus leaves promotes fire. I return to the local park with the keen eye of a young university student, counting the Indian mynas for a group project. The mynas are invasive, brought here by European settlers. Am I like them, I wonder, a foreigner in this land? I receive an eighty for my paper and file it away.

My foliage changes, juvenile branches spreading out, and I discover the world beyond my lecture theatre and local park. I drag myself awake at four am to hear a pre-dawn chorus of eastern yellow robins; I wade through swamps; I clean the microscopic eggs of subantarctic springtails in a climate-

Amy Coetsee

controlled lab. I sew joey pouches, cut fruit for hungry possums, drive for hours to help feed baby wombats. I learn to dive in the cold waters of Melbourne, shivering on the banks of Port Phillip Bay on what is supposed to be a summer's evening. When I finally dive in the Great Barrier Reef, I am lost in the magic of the coral jungle, and cry underwater when I see my first green sea turtle.

I finish my undergraduate degree but want to keep learning. Uncertain about which way to grow, reaching for sunshine, I turn to the eastern barred bandicoot for a while. This species almost became extinct due to invasive predators and habitat loss, but a final few were found in a rubbish tip near Hamilton in the late 1980s. New populations have since been established on three fox-free islands that act as safe havens, protecting them from predation. I fall in love with this small creature, which has one of the shortest pregnancies – just twelve days – of any animal. I learn that bandicoots forage in the dirt for a tasty meal of beetles, spiders, caterpillars and worms, and that their digging keeps the soil healthy, aerated and moist.

I help monitor the populations, luring them into traps with bait made of oats, peanut butter and golden syrup, to check their health before releasing them. Some bandicoots learn the drill – a quick health check in exchange for a free meal – and we find them back in another trap on the same night, happily munching on second helpings of the Anzac-esque treat. My favourite bandicoot is 7B0081E, a female caught one spring with a particular liking for beetles and crickets (and a dream for a bored high-schooler with a calculator). In the lab, I search through their scats. I make my own small discovery – the bandicoots have started eating crabs from the mudflats of Churchill Island! I write my honours thesis, get my mark, and file it away, a little closer to my heart this time.

I know what it is for my people to be oppressed, to be uprooted and killed, separated from their loved ones.

My grandmother fled the German concentration camps to the shores of Australia, a promise of a new life. No family remaining, the eucalypts offered her their generous shade from the sweltering sun, but the flames of Europe never left her.

53

Then I step out into the wilderness, no longer juvenile, not yet a mature tree, seeking Leadbeater's possums and smoky mice, a flash of a tail on a camera, a glimmer of an eye. I cross Eastern Victoria, from Omeo to Mitta Mitta, Mansfield to Wilsons Prom. I climb through gullies and up steep mountains, balancing on fallen logs and falling through detritus. Early-morning dew dampens my khaki pants, and afternoon rainfall drenches them. Camping by the Big River after a long day of work, I see my first platypus in the wild. In my tent, I dream of towering eucalypts.

I am maturing, growing into myself as I begin to flower, swirling patterns bulging on my trunk. I have a symbiotic relationship with the mycorrhizal fungi and the bacteria in the soil. I am Australian by descent, a foreigner here, but I feel at home. Most days, though, I am desperately aware of my invasiveness, making myself comfortable among other intruders in this land – a blackberry bush choking native shrubs, a red fox devouring vulnerable fauna. I mean no harm, but I have spread my roots in Indigenous soil. I am sorry, and I'm here to listen, to follow, and to learn. I want to heal this country together.

I know what it is for my people to be oppressed, to be uprooted and killed, separated from their loved ones. My grandmother fled the German concentration camps to the shores of Australia, a promise of a new life. No family remaining, the eucalypts offered her their generous shade from the sweltering sun, but the flames of Europe never left her.

I think I have grown into an adult eucalypt now, shedding my outermost skin in ribbons, exposing a new layer of fresh, living bark. In a while I will sprout capsule fruiting bodies, drop them to the earth, leave them to germinate in fire and rain. My branches will twist, contorting into woven silhouettes, ancient shapes taking form. One day, when I am a dead stag hollowed out by fire, I will offer shelter to gliders, owls and songbirds, hold them in my caverns. I like to think that Grandma Poss's great-great-grandchildren will call me Home, too.

54

Ella Loeffler is an early-career wildlife ecologist from Melbourne. She holds a double degree in Ecology and Literature and wrote her honours thesis on bandicoot poo. She has worked with endangered species around the world, but Aussie animals are still her favourite. She currently works as a biodiversity policy officer.

Graeme Simsion

Gavin

'Lead poisoning,' says Jim, our local handyman, even before we've walked from his ute to the house. It takes me a moment to realise it's not a diagnosis; it's a treatment. To be administered from the barrel of a gun.

I've asked Jim to take a look at the damage that an animal – almost certainly a wombat – has been wreaking on the foundations of our little weekender in central Victoria, with the idea of building some sort of a fence to keep him out. *Him*: our kids, who've been kept awake by the all-night digging, have, sight unseen, given him a male name.

'Definitely a wombat,' says Jim. He points with the toe of his boot to the scat near our front door. 'Only animal with square shit. So it won't roll off the logs where he leaves it. Supposedly it's to attract a mate.' He crouches and looks at the area under the house, now crisscrossed with deep burrows. 'I suppose it could be two of them under there if it's worked for him. But you've got to wonder what sort of anatomy they've got to make it that shape.'

Bones around the anus is the answer. I've done some reading and I know a little more than I did about this marsupial that is quirky even by marsupial standards. The Victorian poet Dante Gabriel Rossetti kept one as a pet. There's a video simulation of a wombat pipping Usain Bolt over a hundred metres. And the collective noun – if it's ever needed, as they're solitary creatures – is *wisdom*.

As to the single one we're dealing with, it seems that we've got two options, not counting Jim's more direct solution. Dirty up his environment with various

Caleb McElrea

sorts of non-cuboidal droppings – dogs' and chicken's are recommended – or build a fence.

Jim laughs at the 'dirty up' option. 'Got a friend who tried that. Dirtied himself up all right, pushing chicken manure and poo he'd collected from the dog into the burrows, and then they had the smell hanging around for a fortnight. Soon as it was gone, their mate was back. You've got to ask who's the smart one there. And no point in relocating him; it's illegal for a start, and he'll probably get killed by other animals. He's decided this is his territory.'

The fence looks like the only humane solution.

'It's not as simple as it sounds,' says Jim. 'If he wants to get back in, he'll get back in. He'll break through or tunnel under. You'd be amazed. They're digging machines. Built for it. You know their pouch is on back to front so it doesn't get full of dirt?' *Our furry relative of the giant diprotodon with the cuboidal poo is a veritable case study in evolution. And, apparently, bloody-minded persistence.*

Jim lets me know what I'm up for if I pursue the fence option. The mesh will need to be buried thirty centimetres in the ground. Reinforced with star pickets, because thirty centimetres won't be enough to stop a wombat. And he'll need to put in a gate so we still have access. 'One-way, so he can get out if he's still under there when it's finished. We don't want to starve the poor bugger.'

Shooting is still on the agenda, though, and Jim wants this city guy to have a clear-eyed understanding of the situation before he takes my money. 'It's one animal. It's not an orange-bellied parrot. Common wombat, not endangered. And they're a bloody pest. If it was a rabbit or fox or a rat . . . he mimes a rat trap closing. And when you look at it, rats are pretty smart. But you're not going to build a fence to save a rat.'

'Native animal, though.'

'You could say that about a possum. Or a snake. Spider. Where do you draw the line? They're cute animals, but they've got a reputation for being nasty buggers. Like koalas. Bloke I know's kid got bitten by one. Have to say, though, it's usually people's own fault. They're wild animals: leave them alone and they'll leave you alone. This guy's only trying to make a place for himself and we're the ones trying to throw him out.'

'Or kill him.'

'I'm just saying, for the cost of a fence, the logical thing would be to make a donation to a wildlife fund. For endangered animals if you wanted.' He turns over the idea. 'It'd be the logical thing.'

'And shoot this one?'

'Bushfires knock off thousands of them and we're worrying about one that might walk in front of a car the day after we build the fence. I'm not trying to push you one way or the other, just putting it out there.'

Not just an evolutionary case study: a classic problem in ethics – perhaps utilitarian philosophy – probably sleeping a few metres from us. The close one, or the distant many. Two competing but quintessentially human traits: reason, which leads us to the greatest-good response, and empathy, which reinforces our emotional connection with fellow creatures. What did Stalin say – one death is a tragedy; a million is a statistic?

We spend a minute or two pondering these heavy questions. I suspect Jim's enthusiasm for the solution he's proposing is diminishing the longer we talk about our unwanted guest.

'Look,' he says, 'it's your call. I'm happy to take your money: cheaper than having the house fall down. I suppose your kids won't thank you if you pay me to shoot the bugger. You said they'd given him a name?'

'Gavin,' I say.

'Where do you want the gate to go?'

Graeme Simsion is a former IT consultant who decided at fifty to become a writer. The Rosie Project and its sequels, The Rosie Effect and The Rosie Result, have sold over five million copies in forty languages, with movie rights sold to Sony Pictures. The Best of Adam Sharp and Two Steps Forward (written with Anne Buist) have also been international bestsellers with movie rights optioned. Graeme lives in Melbourne with Anne and a cat.

Tom Keneally

Australia's groundkeeper

I got to know echidnas only after I moved to Manly and became an habitué of the wonderful headland scrub of North Head. It is a place where on bush tracks, and sometimes on the street, you encounter them, these well-spurred, spiky balls of spines with what I find to be an amiable snouted face.

The snout is, of course, a bird-like beak to go with the other oddities of the echidna's nature. Something about their humble, defensive imperturbability attracts me. For longer than I like to confess, I mistakenly considered 'echidna' an Aboriginal name, but no, she carries the name of the Mother of Monsters in Greek mythology, the half-human, half-snake woman. The human side of her is suckling, and the snake side of her is the small leathery eggs she lays.

She is an enduring mystery from the other side of the emergence of hominids. I call the echidna 'she' because it's a species in which the females have the best tricks, even if they are tricks not commonly visible to humans. And she doesn't have the crowd-pleasing tricks of her fellow monotreme, the platypus, though we are told she can swim, especially if required to. (Monotreme refers to the one aperture for all functions.)

I say she has the best tricks even while acknowledging that the males have each four penises, two of which they employ at the one time when impregnating a female and two of which they reserve for next time. A line of males will follow the female nose-to-tail for up to a month, tough work in the tangle of North Head, and then she will turn and mate through her

Patrick Tomkins

Kristian Bell

bifurcated genitals with the male who lasts best and is able to neutralise other males with his poisonous spurs.

Within ten days she will lay an egg, dropping it into a body pouch full of milk glands without teats. The egg hatches and the hatchling stays in her pouch until maturity. At hatching it has no hind legs. The small creature is called a 'puggle', a name good enough to satisfy the euphonious wordplay of any child. You don't often see a puggle in the wild, because she strictly keeps the child in her pouch, or, later on, her burrow, and discourages infant adventures.

Most interestingly, she has been found to have REM sleep. The echidna dreams. What is the echidna's dreaming?

On a walk in the bush, on a morning full of the thick, particulate smoke of a burning country, and haunted by the global anxiety we felt that summer, I encountered one of the echidnas threatened, by both the fires and the state of the world, with extinction.

I love this creature: it gives off an air, despite its limited movement, of industry, and has the sort of waddle that in humans is the mark of elderly groundkeepers you have to charm before you're allowed to do anything. As I met her that day, she was turning over the earth to the depth of her beak in her search for provender. It was touching, of course, because she didn't know she was in danger. I watched as always for the flick of her tongue, six to seven inches and lethally sticky to termites.

To see an echidna in the wild bespeaks how much human occupation, a tower of millennia, there has been in Australia, and of the contrast between Indigenous stewards and the stewardship of us immigrant groups. Look at this busy survivor, who has been turning Australian soil for at least 20 million years, and one realises she has seen an unimagined version of our continent, has protected her young from the tread of the diprotodon, from the maws of the thylacine and the carnifex, the lethal marsupial lion, now extinct. And in her august monotreme presence the news comes all the more forcefully that it has taken us less than two and a half centuries to bring the heroically surviving echidna, and the environment that sustains her, to crisis.

She doesn't deserve it.

Name of her species: *Tachyglossus aculeatus*. Fast-tongued spiky. Australia's groundkeeper.

Tom Keneally is the author of more than fifty works of fiction and non-fiction, including *Schindler's Ark*, winner of the Booker Prize, and *The Chant of Jimmie Blacksmith*. He has twice won the Miles Franklin Literary Award (for *Bring Larks and Heroes* and *Three Cheers for the Paraclete*). His most recent novel is *The Dickens Boy*.

63

Patrick Tomkins

Jen Martin

Three Martins and a toadlet

David Attenborough, Beyoncé, Mick Jagger, Marilyn Monroe, Nelson Mandela, John Cleese, Mozart, Greta Thunberg, the Dalai Lama and Rudyard Kipling.

What do these people have in common? They all have animal species named after them. And, for as long as I can remember, I've been deeply proud of the fact that my dad is among their ranks. I was in my final year of primary school when this recognition was bestowed upon him by his colleagues Margaret Davies and Murray Littlejohn. I vividly remember a conversation in which I tried to convince my school friends that having a 'toadlet' (a little grey and yellow frog) named after you was one of the coolest things that could ever happen.

I knew my dad had done a lot of frog-centred field research in exciting places when I was a kid (as evidenced by the postcards he sent my brothers and me), but at that age I don't think I really understood much of what he was doing, or why. Perhaps having a frog named after him signalled to my young self that what he had been doing was both important and valued.

It wasn't until many years later, when I was an undergraduate zoology student, that I thought again about the frog. I found out where it lived and the fact that it was one of very few toadlets to have teeth. I was delighted to discover that the only sure-fire way to tell Martin's toadlet and the closely related Tyler's toadlet apart is by their calls. This seemed fitting, given my dad's

Matt Clancy

close friendship with fellow herpetologist Mike Tyler. It also became clear to me there was a lot we didn't know about Martin's toadlet and that, due to land clearing and drought, its ongoing survival was looking quite uncertain.

I remember asking Dad (who by this time had retired) about the toadlet and discovering that, among the dozens of frog species he'd researched over many years, he had no clear memory of ever meeting 'his' frog. At that point I started hatching a plan to remedy the situation: it seemed essential to me that he should have the opportunity to hold a Martin's toadlet in his hands. But amid a PhD, a busy academic job, marriage and children, I never got around to acting on my impulse.

It took the death, almost twenty years later, of Patsy Littlejohn, Dad's colleague Murray Littlejohn's wife, who was a combined surrogate grandmother and aunt to me, to underline just how precious time is. I didn't want to wait any longer, so I started asking herpetologist friends for help, which revealed that the frog was now of great conservation concern. It had already disappeared from a number of previously consistent monitoring sites; if we were going to find Martin's toadlet, we needed to do it soon.

On the warm, clear afternoon of 18 December 2013, we set off from Melbourne on a three-hour drive to East Gippsland. In the car I was joined by my dad, my then five-year-old son, Rohan, and Nick, a friend, colleague and expert herpetologist. Nearing our destination, we drove along a rough, dusty track and met up with another Rohan, a knowledgeable local ecologist who had identified a perfect spot for our search: an old dam in a stunning patch of forest.

We chatted and wandered as we waited for dusk to arrive. I didn't doubt the expertise of my companions, but I did wonder about our chances of actually finding the frog. The summer had been dry and dusty and, as the sun set, my little dream seemed more and more like a very long shot.

Would it matter if we didn't find one? I think my dad was moved by my passion for the quest, while the ecologists among us were well-accustomed to the disappointment of fruitless searches. My son was simply excited by the adventure with his beloved grandad and the pleasure of knowing that his little sister hadn't been considered old enough to join us. But to me it mattered deeply: for twenty years I had pictured my dad holding 'his' frog and I wasn't sure whether we would have another opportunity like this one if luck didn't favour us this time.

I remember it being a beautiful, still evening, and – sure enough – frogs started calling as soon as darkness fell. It didn't take long for us to recognise the calls of four different species: not including the one we wanted, but it was a promising start. I took my chatterbox son for a walk up the track under the still-pale sky, knowing that the herpetologists needed to be able to listen carefully. I can't recall now what we whispered about, but I do remember my gratitude at being there with him. And I wondered what he would remember of the expedition in the years to come.

Barely any time had passed before I turned and saw three torch-beams being used to triangulate the location of a calling frog. Oh, the anticipation – had they really found a Martin's toadlet? To my joy: yes! One, and only one, tiny grey and yellow toadlet had announced his presence with a characteristic second-long 'aaaaaaaaaaaaaaaaaaaaarrr'.

In the years since, I have thought back to that night so many times – helped by the fact we have a picture on our wall from the evening, of my dad with my son and I on either side of him. We are all staring down at his hands and you have to look carefully to see the tiny frog he is gently holding. Each of us has a different expression on our face: my dad is clearly proud, I have a big grin, and my son, tenderly holding his grandfather's hand, has a look of innocence and wonder that still brings tears to my eyes.

Of course, we released the frog immediately after we had photographed him, and he had already started calling again by the time we drove off into the starry night, all smiling. Martin's toadlet is thought to be quite long-lived, so it's conceivable that the same little frog is still around today, with no idea of the central role he played in making my dream come true.

I'm trying not to think about what the January 2020 bushfires might have meant for Martin's toadlet – to be honest, I've been too afraid to ask. But I'll never forget that night and the sense of quiet fulfilment and gratitude I felt and still feel today.

On the long drive home, just before dozing off, little Rohan (who is now taller than I am) said: 'That's one of the best things that's ever happened to me.' I couldn't have said it better myself.

Dr Jen Martin spent many years working as a field ecologist until she decided the most useful thing she could contribute as a scientist was to teach other scientists how to be effective and engaging communicators. Jen founded and leads the University of Melbourne's acclaimed Science Communication Teaching Program. Jen also practises what she preaches: she's been talking about science each week on 3RRR radio for fifteen years, writes for a variety of publications, MCs events and was named the Unsung Hero of Australian Science Communication for 2019.

Geraldine Brooks

Arachnophilia

Don't worry, spiders,
I keep house
casually

—Kobayashi Issa, b. 1763

I'm looking at him. He's looking back.

He's looking down, in fact, from the ceiling of my bedroom. His eight-eyed stare is the last thing I see each night before I reach over and turn off the light.

But in the dark, he's still looking. I can't see him now, but I know he sees me. He has better night vision than I have.

I always imagined that his superfluity of eyes would enable him to see the world in vivid, sparkling beauty – more colours, more details. But scientists say that's not so. His eyes are arrayed in two rows of four simply so that he can sense movement, trap prey. The internal structures of his eyes are of the type that give only blurry, wide-angled images.

All those eyes – the row of four on top of his head and the row of four facing forward – are the most alien, perhaps the most alienating, thing about him. Eight legs? No big deal. We live with animals who have more legs than we do. We're used to that. But when we gaze into a dog's eyes, or a cat's, they gaze back at us with a familiar stare, eyeball to eyeball. It's easy to befriend them. It's one of the attributes that makes them easy to love.

Nick Porch

Loving a huntsman spider, of the family Sparassidae (from the Greek, to rip or tear), is, perhaps, a bigger ask. But when you live in the inner city, wildlife is scarce, elusive. So you need to appreciate what you have. The huntsman spider on my bedroom ceiling is not my pet, but he is my housemate. His ancestors were on this bit of rocky Sydney harbourside long before mine were. Why should I not welcome him?

I do welcome him, in fact. I assume he is male, because I have seen no egg sacs, and huntsman egg sacs can be conspicuously large – some, I've read, the size of ping-pong balls.

He is a graceful creature, an athlete. He's built for speed. He's faster than the best of human runners. Usain Bolt, for example, can travel five body lengths per second. A huntsman spider has been clocked at forty-two. Because of this swiftness, he is relieved of the necessity to spin a web. If a mosquito lands, he feels the vibration and runs down his prey with lethal speed.

Is he cute? I think so. He is pleasantly furred. He is polite and moves away when he senses that is required. But he can also be clingy. Once you have him on your hand, it can be hard to convince him to let go. When I have had occasion to touch him – once, for instance, to move him out of sight of a hyperventilating arachnophobic guest – he was light in my hand, and soft as a feather. He isn't an itsy-bitsy spider. He's as big as my palm. He has venom, I know this, but it's not very toxic to humans. I also know that his jaws are too small, his fangs insufficient, to easily puncture human skin. Even so, I move slowly, so as not to startle him. Generally, we give each other our space.

The huntsman spider on my bedroom ceiling is not my pet, but he is my housemate. His ancestors were on this bit of rocky Sydney harbourside long before mine were. Why should I not welcome him?

There are 1207 species of huntsman spider in the world. You can find 155 of them in Australia, and most of these can't be found anywhere else. Some species have grand and violent names, Goliath, Hercules, that refer to their size and not their shy nature. David Bowie has a species named after him, a Malaysian huntsman with a shock of yellow hair.

My resident huntsman is no rock star, no mythical hero. His furry head and legs are subtly toned with the soft greys and beiges of his native habitat, the dry sclerophyll forests of the Sydney foreshore. My terrace house also has a muted colour palette, which is maybe why he feels at home here. I think, but am not sure, that he is a *Delena cancerides*, a 'social huntsman'. *Cancerides* comes from his supposed crab-like movement, but I don't think he moves like a crab at all. I think he moves like a dancer, swift and lithe, graceful and powerful.

And because of him, there are no mosquitos in my bedroom. It's been years since I've seen a cockroach. But more than that: he brings the wilderness inside my house.

Thank you, friend.

Geraldine Brooks won the Pulitzer Prize for Fiction in 2006 for her novel *March*. Her novels *The Secret Chord*, *Caleb's Crossing* and *People of the Book* were *New York Times* bestsellers. Her first novel, *Year of Wonders*, was an international bestseller, translated into more than twenty-five languages. She is also the author of the non-fiction works *Nine Parts of Desire*, *Foreign Correspondence* and *The Idea of Home*. She lives with a horse, a dog and as much wildlife as possible.

Nick Porch

Consider the little things

I remember that day, twenty-five years ago, in the heart of Gippsland. I can still picture a tree-fern glade, deep within a forest remnant I called Lyrebird Gully. Not an official name, but for as long as I can remember there were always lyrebirds calling, building their groomed mounds, and leaving feathers to go in vases on the mantelpiece. Back then, before the seeds of my obsession with beetles had been sown, I still tended to notice the big things. Showy things. The ones that made the most noise.

I don't recall seeing any lyrebirds on that day back in 1994. They may have been about, strutting around. Perhaps I had become inured to their charms, if that was even remotely possible. I'd dipped down off the road, through the roadside thicket, tripping and tumbling as usual. The slopes were steep. South-Gippsland steep. The descent was equal parts sliding on my rear and a technique involving purposeful falling. Choose a small tree just below, a hazel pomaderris, an austral mulberry, or maybe a tree lomatia. It needs to be close enough to arrest momentum before it builds too much, but distant enough that you make some headway. Take a step down the slope: already descending too quickly, palm the cool bark to stop. Thanks, elderberry panax, I've never noticed you here! Scout, choose another tree nearby, and repeat.

The slope became even steeper ahead of me. A forgotten landslide scarp. Below, a fairy glade, but home to something even more magical. Soft tree ferns, green-dripping, filmy-ferned trunks, blue sky between streaming fronds.

Slide down the scarp into a little paradise. Mud-stained pants. All pants are beetling pants. Deep, musty leaf litter. Rotting, pithy. Giant gurgling worms and the muddy castles of burrowing crayfish. Wetter there. Reached a dry fern frond and rested for a bit, with leeches finding sustenance between my toes. Too many. Time to work again.

What brings all this back is a jaundiced beetle pinned in a box, surrounded by thirty-seven other specimens, all from that afternoon in the ferny glade. There's more to Lyrebird Gully than lyrebirds and momentum-arresting trees. I haven't even mentioned the mountain ash, biggest of the big things. Ignore them for a minute and consider the little things. I wonder how many people like to go for a walk, lie down with the leeches, spread the leaf litter and gawp at the unknown multitudes. Would they know what they are seeing? Would they marvel at it?

I look at that beetle now with fresh eyes. Look harder. Ponder. I need Moore's *A Revision of the Australian Trechinae*, almost forty years old. It is in the cabinet, filled with slowly fading glossy reprints and photocopies with rusty staples, the literature of a world of wonders. But only if you know how to see. No field guides to the hidden, parallel world of beetles. To see, really see, I need a microscope, and to know whether the mentum is concave, and fused to the throat-like gula. Indeed, it is, among other things. Looks like a *Tropidotrechus*. Moore's paper tells me there are four species of this beetle, all only found in and around the wet forests of Victoria's Central Highlands. Nowhere near Lyrebird Gully. That should have spurred me to look closer, but I placed the beetle back in the box for another decade or so. I'm guilty of not seeing well enough. It turns out, I realised recently, it's a new species of *Tropidotrechus*, still only known from that locality, which is surrounded by encroaching hardwood plantations. It might still be there in future for someone to formally name. Hopefully, it won't only be remembered by the single pallid specimen I collected, on a lovely afternoon in 1994.

Recently, I was in the Dandenongs, easier country for an older body. Pound Creek, flowing down towards Puffing Billy's home turf. This is the territory

I wonder how many people like to go for a walk, lie down with the leeches, spread the leaf litter and gawp at the unknown multitudes. Would they know what they are seeing?

of *Tropidotrechus victoriae*; no common name now and probably forever. It would be Victoria's official invertebrate emblem, if we had one. I had never seen one alive, just a few old specimens in the museum, collected almost a hundred years ago, but now I was chasing a picture of a living one. Fern-glade memories meant I headed straight for the bottom of the gully. Eventually I reached tree-fern shade. Long-legged craneflies hanging from fronds. Cool litter. Perfect habitat for the beetle I was searching for.

For a couple of hours, nothing. Well, not nothing. Quick little rove-beetles; the ubiquitous landhoppers; red velvet mites; cool, slow *Hypoponera* ants; and springtails, everywhere springtails. Footsteps in the mud beside the creek. Gosh. The only time I've come across evidence of people in these deeper gullies. Looking for beetles? Unlikely, but you never know. I am. Turn over rotting dead wood, scan and replace. My eyes aren't what they once were. Try another, this time larger, and a beautifully patterned shining fungus beetle sits still for a picture. That's new to me. A streak of a beetle, burrowing into a crack in the wood. A ground beetle. The right group. Yellowish, I think, but quick. About half a fingernail wide. Look closer and there's another standing still. These things never stay still! Camera, two quick pictures and it's gone.

While I still notice the big things, as we all should, I've learnt to love the little things.

Dr Nick Porch is a South Gippslander and Senior Lecturer in Environmental Earth Science at Deakin University, where he studies human impact on Indo-Pacific island invertebrate biodiversity, and the rich, unique and understudied Australian beetle fauna. He has four Victorian beetles and a spider named after him. So far.

Paul
Kelly

'Sleep, Australia, Sleep'

'Sleep, Australia, Sleep' is a lament in the form of a lullaby. Paradoxically, it can also be heard as a wake-up call – a critique of the widespread attitude among humans that we are the most important life form on the planet, an attitude that is doing much damage to our world. In the video that goes with the song we highlight some of the many people and organisations who are doing good, effective work. There is plenty we can all do and many ways to help.

—PK

Paul Kelly AO is one of Australia's best loved songwriters. Since giving his first live performance in 1974, he has released twenty-three studio albums. He is the author of *How to Make Gravy*, and compiled the poetry anthology *Love Is Strong as Death*. In 2019 he released *Songs from the South: Paul Kelly's Greatest Hits*. His album *Thirteen Ways to Look at Birds* brings together musicians from broad-ranging backgrounds to interpret bird-inspired poems. His latest release is 'Please Leave Your Light On', with Paul Grabowsky.

Sleep, Australia, sleep
The night is on the creep
Shut out the noise all around
Sleep, Australia, sleep
And dream of counting sheep
Jumping in fields coloured brown

Who'll rock the cradle and cry?
Who'll rock the cradle and cry?
Sleep, Australia, sleep
As off the cliff the kingdoms leap
Count them as they say goodbye
Count down the little things
The insects and birds
Count down the bigger things
The flocks and the herds
Count down our rivers
Our pastures and trees
But there's no need to hurry
Oh, sleep now, don't worry
'Cos it's only a matter of degrees

Fog, Australia, fog
Just like the boiling frog
As we go we won't feel a thing

Who'll rock the cradle and cry?
Who'll rock the cradle and cry?
Sleep, my country, sleep
As off the cliff the kingdoms leap
Count them as they pass on by

Our children might know them
But their children will not
We won't know 'til it's gone
All the glory we've got
But there are more
  wonders coming
All new kinds of shows
With acid seas rising
To kiss coastal mountains
Big cyclones pounding
And firestorms devouring
And we'll lose track of counting
As the corpses keep mounting
But, hey, that's just the way
  this old world goes

Sleep, my country, sleep
As we sow so shall we reap
Who'll rock the cradle and cry?

Water

Sonia Orchard

A moment at sea

The water was inky blue and choppy. Waves spilt over onto the nearby reef. I rode up and down on the swell, hunched over, with the other guests lined up along the marlin board. I wasn't feeling too much excitement; I was concentrating on not being sick.

Given the word, I launched off from the boat, then sat buoyed up in the ocean while icy fingers wormed their way up my wetsuit. Our guide called out again, pointing away from the reef, towards the horizon.

I dipped my mask and snorkel into the water and looked along the surface. And there it was. Appearing mostly as an outline, grainy blue in the sun-dappled, plankton-speckled water: a submarine heading towards us. Then the dark blur in the centre – the oblong mouth – came into resolution. A metre-wide slit, open and drawing in water. As it moved closer, silently, tiny eyes appeared on either side of its mouth, seemingly oblivious to the minute creatures flitting around in front of it. I quickly finned out of its path – it wasn't about to adjust its course for anyone. Not that it looked sinister – well, not at first – with an almost comical-looking head and a torso you just wanted to run your hands along, patterned with grey and white stripes and spots. But then moments later, as it moved effortlessly past, the unmistakable, shudder-inducing silhouette of a shark.

Whale sharks are the largest fish in the ocean, and grow to around the size and weight of a bus. But unlike most other sharks, the whale shark is a filter feeder, consuming only plankton and small fish. They are the true gentle giant.

I'd wanted to swim with whale sharks for decades, ever since I first snorkelled with minke whales in my twenties. I remember lying still at the surface for over an hour as two whales, a mother and calf, circled me, inching closer and closer until I could have almost touched them. Each time one glided past, its large eyes – unmistakably mammalian – locked on mine. So soft, so curious, so different to the empty gaze of a fish. I felt like I was gazing deep into the eyes of a human trapped inside a giant whale suit.

I was working as a diving instructor on the Great Barrier Reef at the time, and became used to seeing people emerge from the water after swimming with minke whales, manta rays or whale sharks, unable to really articulate what had happened, wandering about the back deck with an idiotic grin, still spouting superlatives hours later. I knew exactly how that felt.

This experience, of feeling small and humbled in the presence of something vast and beyond immediate understanding, is now thought to be vital to human wellbeing.

Humans are hardwired to respond strongly to animals. Recent research indicates that there are neurons within the amygdala – the brain's seat of emotions – that fire when a person sees any kind of animal, but that don't react as strongly to the sight of a person, place or object. It's thought that this response evolved in our prehominid ancestors, when they lived on the African savanna millions of years ago and needed to be hyper-alert to any animals appearing in the distance. Although this ancient alarm system is rarely needed by modern humans, the sight of an animal still triggers a powerful emotional reaction. And if the creature isn't a threatening one, that intense tickling of the amygdala makes us feel good.

Interacting with an animal like a whale shark or a minke whale also induces another positive emotion: awe. This experience, of feeling small and humbled in the presence of something vast and beyond immediate understanding, is now thought to be vital to human wellbeing. Awe can give rise to an almost transcendental happiness not found in individual successes and their rewards, but in their exact opposite: feeling insignificant, a self dissolved into the whole. After experiencing awe, people have been found to behave more altruistically and report increased levels of contentedness. There are also signs that awe may have benefits for the immune system.

It was three years ago when I swam with the whale sharks, twenty-five years ago when I eyeballed the minke whale mother and calf. These days, I spend most of my hours not bobbing around at sea, but inside a house staring into the glow of a computer screen, trying to fill it with words, in between ushering kids out the door in the morning and welcoming them back in the afternoon, then heading into the after-school extreme sport we call modern-day parenting. But during the day there are sulphur-crested cockatoos that interrupt my work, cackling from the eucalypts outside my window, and if I stumble upon an online video of a cat, goat, dolphin or baby elephant, that can sometimes be enough – I can say goodbye to the next half hour. It's just too addictive. That feeling of being humbled. That feeling of being amazed.

Sonia Orchard is the author of three books: a memoir, *Something More Wonderful*, and the novels *The Virtuoso* (winner of the 2009 Indie Book Award for Best Debut Fiction) and *Into the Fire*. She also writes non-fiction and opinion pieces on a variety of issues, from the environment to gender politics. She has degrees in music, literature and environmental science, and a PhD in creative writing.

Robbie Arnott

The leap

W hen it reveals itself, we aren't ready. My cousin and I are swaying
on the deck of my uncle's boat, rods straight, lines wet. We're facing
south, away from the navy field of Bass Strait and towards West Head, a vast
extrusion of dolerite cliffs that rise from the water on the edge of Narawntapu
National Park. To the cliffs' east lies the broad mouth of the Tamar River; to
the west, a long blonde beach, and, beyond it, more cliffs and headlands and
sand until another river breaks free into the strait. Then the shark leaps.

It is so fast, so sudden. We are sun-drunk and slow, waiting for the pulse of
a flathead bite, and then the sea is broken by a surging flash of colour. The
creature rises from the water at monstrous speed, right in front of my cousin
and me. It climbs from the surface, shaking off the ocean's grip – a total
breach. The animal hangs there, held by air. A blue-grey back, a white belly.
Sloped fins. A sickled tail, at least as long as its torpedo of a body. Rising
muscle. Flying death. A thresher shark.

My father and uncle are at the front of the boat, so they don't see it. My
cousin and I are the only witnesses. Behind the sea-freed shark are waters
that we know with intimacy. For our whole lives we have paddled these
waves, ridden their rips. We've been pulling fish from their depths for as long
as we can remember: flathead and cocky salmon, to be breaded and shallow-
fried, and gasping gurnards and countless wrasse, to be underarmed back.
With snorkels strapped we've prised blacklip abalone from sheltered reefs

Heather Sutton

and, further out, greenlips from rocks exposed to colder currents. We've seen the black shadows of stingrays speeding across the pale sea floor. We've watched the swirling patterns of cuttlefish flesh. We've smelt the huff of seal breath; we've tasted squid ink sprayed across our faces.

But we've never seen a shark fly.

Its leap does not contain enough time for us to speak. We can only watch as the thresher rises higher, propelled by a thrash of its scything tail. Later, when I look the species up, I learn that they don't just use their tails to breach – they use them to hunt. The shark will swim directly at a school of smaller fish, tail poised, before braking suddenly by twisting its pectoral fins. This causes the front half of its body to dip and its back half to rise, positioning the tail in a trebuchet-like motion, before the shark whips it forward into the school. If it connects directly, it will kill its prey on impact, sometimes even slicing the fish into pieces. If it misses, the tail generates enough force to create an explosive pressure-wave powerful enough to stun its prey cold. The shark can then circle around, lazily snapping up the dazed or eviscerated fish in its short, toothy mouth.

The creature rises from the water at monstrous speed. It climbs from the surface, shaking off the ocean's grip –

In the air, the initial grace of the shark's leap has deserted it. Gravity has loosened its pose, pulling its fins and body back towards the water. Only the tail remains high, at the peak of its propelling whip. It's not clear why thresher sharks breach. It could be part of their hunting behaviour – the crash of their body reconnecting with the surface might shock or disorient their prey – or they could fly for the simple thrill of it. It's possible they just enjoy the sensation of dry air on their ever-wet cartilage.

a total breach. The animal hangs there, held by air. A blue-grey back, a white belly. Sloped fins. A sickled tail, at least as long as its torpedo of a body.

What is known is that this behaviour is a threat to their survival. Rising so abruptly into the sky has earned the thresher shark the attention of the sports fishing industry – people like to watch it leap on the end of a line. Some fish are killed; some are returned; some are unintentionally maimed and left to slowly

Rising muscle.

Flying death.

A thresher shark.

die. Like so many other shark species, threshers are already under pressure. Overfishing and the degradation of their food chain, combined with their low rate of reproduction, has seen their numbers sharply fall over the last few decades. Now, they are hunted for fun. There is no evidence of unprovoked thresher sharks ever being a danger to humans.

As our shark descends to rejoin the ocean, I finally let out a sound – a yelp of strangled awe. Or perhaps it is my cousin who makes the noise; later on, we cannot remember which of us it was. My father and uncle turn around, but it is too late. By the time they're facing the cliffs, the shark is gone. All that remains is a splash of foam. What was that? they ask. Was it a seal? A dolphin? A school of salmon?

Staring at the air the shark had occupied, we try to tell them. We try to explain what we've seen. And while we can say the words *shark* and *leap* and *incredible*, we can't articulate what has happened – what has been revealed, and then so quickly taken away. We can't explain that we are now, in ways both small and huge, changed. We can't tell them the sea has torn its face apart to show us the truth of its wildness. We can only stare, and mumble, and sway on the waves beneath the high dark cliffs.

Robbie Arnott is the author of *Flames*, which won the 2019 Margaret Scott Prize and was shortlisted and longlisted for many other awards. His latest novel, *The Rain Heron*, was released in June 2020. He lives in Tasmania.

Meg Keneally

The fellow traveller

He barrels at me out of the dimness, his contours resolving as he gets closer. I think his momentum will carry him right past me, even against the force of the current, and it seems for a moment that it nearly does. But this is his element. At the last second he turns sharply, maintaining his glide, until his face is centimetres from mine.

He is still, for a short while, only his pectoral fins moving, quite lazily. He seems inquisitive, although he's seen more and more of my kind in the few decades he has probably been alive.

I know he's male because of his vibrant shade of blue; not the muted green of a juvenile, not the red-tinged brown of a female, even though he would have started life as one. They all do.

He might be expecting me to cut up an urchin for him, as divers sometimes do. If so, he's out of luck. He may be my favourite creature here, but I won't kill another animal for him.

Anyway, he's perfectly capable of acquiring his own urchin. They're everywhere down here. Their brittle black spines don't seem to bother eastern blue gropers. They nose the urchins over, eating out the animal, crunching up shell and spine with peg-like teeth. More than once, a blue groper has hovered in front of me, opened its mouth and ejected a stream of urchin detritus.

You might think this fish would leave when it becomes apparent I'm not going to help him to an easy meal. I know he probably won't. I start to kick

Sue Liu

my fins, slowly propelling myself forward, and he keeps pace with me for a little while before disappearing from view.

I know it's likely he's still close by. I've seen others like him weaving between divers' fins. If a blue groper takes an interest in you, it's not uncommon for it to follow you for twenty minutes or more. You will know it's there when you try to photograph another species and find a blue head entering the frame just as you press the button. When you see movement under a rock and stop to look, it's not unusual to find a groper wedging itself into the space beside you. When I taught scuba diving, I would sometimes have an extra, blue student watching as I scrawled instructions on my underwater slate.

I try not to anthropomorphise the creatures I meet down here – it seems arrogant – but it's hard with blue gropers (which are not gropers but wrasse, the misnomer being the least of the wrongs my species has done to his). It's easy to interpret their inquisitiveness as friendliness. Anyone who thinks fish don't have personality has never met *Achoerodus viridis*.

This blue groper lives at Cabbage Tree Bay, opposite Manly Beach in New South Wales, in Gayemagal waters. It's a marine park, teeming with life. Students used to ask me what the huge fish that looked just like a flathead was. What they had seen was a flathead that had been allowed to live its life.

I breathed underwater for the first time here, surfacing to ask my instructors why they had been keeping this incredible secret for so long. A short time earlier, kneeling on the sea floor, one of my instructors had pounded his fist into the palm of his hand, and a blue streak came zooming towards us, examining each of us in turn. I've heard people refer to this as 'summoning' the fish, a word I'm not entirely comfortable with despite the great gift I received that day. I remember the orange zigzags around the fish's eyes, and the answering spark I fancied I saw when I looked into them.

There is more than enough to marvel at for several lifetimes. But I am ever so slightly sad after the rare dive when I don't see a blue groper. When one does accompany me for a while, I experience an odd mixture of guilt and yearning when I ascend along the anchor chain of a boat, looking down to see it still circling below.

During most of the dives I've done since, blue gropers have been fellow travellers. They have floated beside me as I gazed at other creatures (after we'd finished gazing at each other). I've drawn comfort from them as they swam next to me in low visibility, or strong currents. They have been a feature of most of the memorable experiences I've had beneath the surface of the harbour or the Tasman Sea.

Sydney's waters conceal an extraordinary range of creatures. Some estimates put the number at nearly 600 fish species, more than are found in the Mediterranean. Non-diving friends are surprised when I show them images of giant cuttlefish – highly intelligent cephalopods capable of changing colour, raising tabs on their mantle and crinkling their tentacles to blend in with the kelp. Or of spotted, elongated weedy sea dragons, cousins of the seahorse.

There are several species of shark, from spotted wobbegongs to Port Jackson sharks to grey nurse sharks, which waft around at places like Long Reef in Sydney's north. There are marine mammals, such as New Zealand fur seals, which laze around on rocks and cavort underwater, and dolphins, which sometimes followed the dive boat I used to work on. Nudibranches, colourful sea slugs, are dotted around the seascape like tiny gems, at the base of soft corals such as orange and yellow sea fans, or mace-like purple sea tulips.

There is more than enough to marvel at for several lifetimes. But I am ever so slightly sad after the rare dive when I don't see a blue groper. When one does accompany me for a while, I experience an odd mixture of guilt and yearning when I ascend along the anchor chain of a boat, looking down to see it still circling below.

Here at Cabbage Tree Bay, there's no need for a boat. You simply swim towards shore until you run out of ocean. When I have a little more than half a tank, I turn, and the fish turns with me. He doesn't seem to want to retrace our route for long, though, and after a few minutes he aims himself at the rocky reef behind me, and disappears back into the greyness with a few balletic fin-flicks. I hang in the water for a moment, hoping he'll come back, but he has urchins to find.

Perhaps people are right when they talk about summoning. But if one of us is summoning the other, I am the one answering the call.

Meg Keneally is the author of *Fled* and *The Wreck*. Together with Tom Keneally, she is also the co-author of the Monsarrat series, murder mysteries set in colonial Australia (*The Soldier's Curse*, *The Unmourned*, *The Power Game* and *The Ink Stain*).

Jayne Jenkins

Karen Viggers

Crabeater seals in Antarctica

A ntarctica is the last great wilderness: a land of endless ice and white light. My father's lifelong interest in Antarctic exploration imbued the place with a magical quality for me. Dad said Scott was a dreamer, Amundsen an organiser, and Shackleton a hero because he never lost a man despite several disasters on his Antarctic expeditions.

I had the unique opportunity to visit Antarctica with the Australian Antarctic Division as a volunteer veterinarian in October 1995. I left Hobart on the bright-orange *Aurora Australis*, slipping past shadowy Bruny Island at dusk and heading into the mountainous swells of the Southern Ocean. I was not a good sailor. The first few days, I lay in my bunk, popping Travacalm tablets and nibbling crackers and Vegemite. When I developed sea legs, I ensconced myself on the ship's bridge, watching seabirds drift past: elegant albatrosses gliding over the waves, their wingtips skimming the water; chunky Cape petrels hitching a ride on the wind; storm-petrels and snow-petrels diving into a krill swarm, kicked up by the ship's churning wake.

Icebergs appeared in the inky water. Then pancake ice: frosted dinner-plate discs that swished against the sides of the ship, dampening the swell. When we reached the pack ice, it was time for the crabeater seal team to start work. After too many lazy days watching movies and playing cards, I was thrown into shipboard and helicopter surveys – trying to separate shadow seals from real ones hauled out on ice floes.

Colin Southwell

Colin Southwell

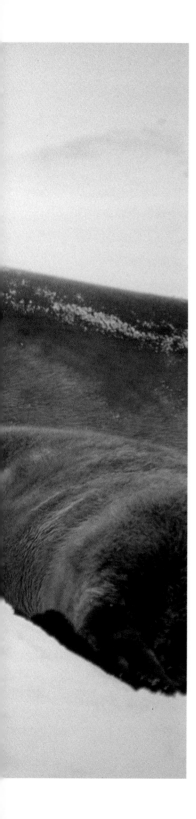

Crabeater seals don't eat crabs, they mostly eat krill. They're beautiful, silver-furred creatures weighing up to 300 kilograms. In breeding season, each pregnant female hauls out onto an ice floe to give birth. There, she off-loads her high-fat milk to her offspring for four to six weeks until weaning. Eventually an adult male seal will find her. He'll hang around on the same floe, waiting until she's too weak to repel his advances. Then he'll separate mother from pup so he can mate with the female. It's not a very romantic breeding strategy, but it's effective. Crabeater seals are the most abundant species of Antarctic seal, with a population of about 15 million. They're dependent on sea ice for their breeding cycle.

Part of our work was to sedate seals and attach satellite trackers to the fur on their backs, so scientists could study their diving and haul-out behaviour. It was tricky but exhilarating work. Once a seal had been selected as a suitable candidate, our small seal-catching team was lowered onto the ice from the ship, or dropped onto a floe from a helicopter. It was a strange feeling when the ship or helicopter moved away, and we were alone in a vast field of crumpled floes, with sky and ice stretching all around. In the stillness, silence took on a new dimension. Within long moments of quiet, the wind sighed around hummocks and castles of rafted ice. When I moved, my crampon spikes crunched in the snow.

To catch a crabeater seal, we had to dart it, which was an imprecise science. We needed to guess the body weight – which was difficult when we'd only seen these seals at a distance from above the ship's bridge. The next steps were to calculate a dose, draw it up with gloved fingers, insert the dart into the rifle, grovel close without scaring the seal, and then fire the dart. When it struck, we then had to work hard to prevent the seal from entering the water. If the animal was to fall asleep down in the icy blue depths, it might die. It was a stressful operation. We wanted the seal to become sedated slowly. But they are wild creatures. More often they would spin frantically, snorting vaporous puffs into the air while they sought a way to escape.

Our first seal was an adult female with a pup. She shifted in sinuous turns, watching us closely until the drug began to grip. Her pup huddled alongside her, darker in colour, with spectacles of brown fur, a floppy-skinned miniature of its mother. As the adult seal quietened down, we moved closer. She was a stunning animal. Domed silvery head, black watery eyes, narrow upturned nose with slit nostrils and cream-coloured prickly whiskers. She had two parallel brown streaks down her side: most likely scars from a leopard seal attack when she was young. Around her mouth were pink stains from her last krill meal, eaten weeks ago, before her pup was born.

Her eyes closed as she relaxed. I slid a bag over her head to reduce stimuli. The wary pup slithered away and hovered at the edge of the floe. He had never been parted from his mother before. Gloves off, I laid a hand on the seal's back to feel the texture of her fur: coarse and strong, velvety and dense underneath. I set up monitoring equipment to check her oxygenation levels, while one of our team took measurements. Another assistant mixed Araldite in an esky, where a hot water bottle prevented the glue from setting too quickly. We swiped the sticky grey muck onto the animal's back and settled the tracker in position. For the next few months that device would transmit data to a satellite until it was shed with the animal's annual moult – an expensive piece of equipment would eventually find its resting place at the bottom of the Southern Ocean. The seal's recovery took almost thirty minutes, while we kept our distance and blocked her exit routes to the sea. When she'd reunited with her pup

Creative and effective ways of saving our fellow creatures on this planet have already been developed by scientists. But to enact real change, all of us need to be like Antarctic adventurers: dreamers, organisers and heroes. It isn't too late.

and seemed safe, we radioed the ship and arranged to be picked up. It was labour-intensive, time-consuming work. But how else can you learn about a cryptic species?

Twenty-five years ago, the crabeater seal's sea-ice habitat and krill diet weren't under immediate threat. But things have changed. In the past decade, the surface area of Antarctic sea ice has been shrinking. Krill stocks have declined too, with major implications for the Antarctic food chain and ecosystem, which is dependent on krill for food. If we don't reduce our carbon emissions and limit the extent of global warming, then at some stage in the future there will be no pack ice and we will lose crabeater seals and many other Antarctic creatures.

Those early Antarctic explorers my father told me about, who captured my imagination when I was young, were sometimes forced to eat seals and penguins to survive. Humans can be adept at finding solutions, albeit imperfect ones, when they are in desperate situations. Creative and effective ways of saving our fellow creatures on this planet have already been developed by scientists. But to enact real change, all of us need to be like Antarctic adventurers: dreamers, organisers and heroes. It isn't too late.

Karen Viggers is a wildlife veterinarian who has worked with native animals in many remote parts of Australia, and in Antarctica. She is passionate about the conservation and restoration of Australian landscapes and wildlife, and uses fiction to explore complex and controversial environmental issues. Karen is the award-winning, internationally bestselling author of *The Stranding*, *The Lightkeeper's Wife*, *The Grass Castle* and *The Orchardist's Daughter*.

Sue Pillans

Drawn to the biggest shark in the sea

M y heart is beating so fast – I'm full of nerves and anticipation. I'm on my
tippy-toes trying to get a glimpse, and then I hear:

'It's 200 metres away at two o'clock.'

'It's a big one, probably close to seven metres.'

'It's now a hundred metres away at three o'clock.'

'Jump in . . . *now!*'

In all the excitement I forget to breathe, but I jump into the ocean anyway.
As the bubbles clear, after looking around, I turn to find a *big* white shape
behind me. Out of the vast blueness emerges what looks like the biggest smile
you have ever seen, followed by an enormous and beautiful whale shark.

Swimming steadily along like a spotted submarine, it comes right towards me.

For a moment, I'm in shock and awe of this incredible creature. In my
excitement I forget that I'm underwater and swallow sea water through my
snorkel. I try to compose myself and watch as the whale shark gracefully
glides right past me. I snap out of my trance and kick as fast as I can to keep
up and swim eye to eye with the shark. I feel oddly connected to this creature,
as though it can peer right inside me, with eyes that must have seen so much
in its lifetime of swimming across our oceans.

The whale shark is covered in a mosaic of spots and stripes so bright it
looks like it is glowing. Even though all of my energy is now consumed with
keeping up with the shark, I get so distracted by this amazing animal that I

Richard Pillans

have to remind myself to 'just keep swimming'. I don't want to miss a single second with this magnificent creature, so I swim as quickly as possible. Then, without warning, the whale shark dives effortlessly into the depths, its body gleaming as it descends into the darkness below. As I make my way back to the boat, I'm smiling – I am full of so many emotions – but mostly I feel a sense of calmness, even though I just swam with the biggest shark in the sea. The smile stays on my face for days.

That was my first whale shark experience and even though it was ten years ago, I can still remember every single detail about that day. Five years later, I found myself part of a marine research team, swimming with whale sharks at Ningaloo Reef in Western Australia, a once-in-a-lifetime opportunity for me. The research focused on attaching satellite tags to whale sharks to find out where these mysterious creatures go. They are a protected species in Australia, and their movements, despite their huge size and regular presence at Ningaloo Reef, are mostly unknown once they leave this aggregation site.

One day I swam with nine whale sharks, which was both exhilarating and exhausting as they can swim at an average leisurely speed of three kilometres per hour. Among these whale sharks was the largest one I have ever seen, a nine-metre-long animal we named Winston. He cruised by us in the water, as if he had somewhere very important to go, which was probably finding his next meal of plankton. I swam with Winston for what seemed like a long time but was in fact less than five minutes.

Big whale sharks like Winston tend to swim nonchalantly in a straight line, making measuring them quite easy. But it was an effort to keep up with him and, with my legs burning, I eventually fell behind. From that angle I got to watch his giant tail sway from side to side in mesmerising movement. Winston was then tagged, and continued to swim with us until he eventually dived down into the dark blue water below. Where did he go, how far did he dive and when would he return to Ningaloo Reef? These were some of the questions we were trying to answer as we kept track of Winston's movements over the next year.

There is a lot we don't know about whale sharks, but it's probable they live for over a century. So it is more than likely that Winston is still gliding under the waves.

Shortly after this experience, I met a whale shark at the other end of the size spectrum. This 'little fella' was about three metres long and he looked and acted differently to all the other whale sharks I'd encountered. As soon as I swam up beside him he became very inquisitive and started following me around, like a big puppy dog, perhaps wondering where my spots and stripes were. I tried to swim away to keep my distance, but each time I did I found myself face to face with him. The curious nature smaller whale sharks often display meant they tended to circle around us, making it hard to measure them. At one stage this little shark was so close to me that I had to hold my legs up to let him swim underneath. I squealed and giggled, filling my mask up with water. This shark was too small to tag.

I have fallen utterly in love with these gentle giants of the sea and I will cherish these encounters forever. As a marine scientist, artist and author I have always been drawn to nature, and whale sharks fascinate me for so many reasons – their enormous size and placid nature, and because they are such mysteries to us. For example, we still don't know where the majority go year round, how long they live for, how fast they grow, where they give birth and how many babies they have. How can an animal that is so big and beautiful have so many unknowns?

This raises even more questions about the whale shark's future, particularly in the face of climate change and increasing human–animal interactions, and the impacts of activities such as fishing, plastic pollution and boat strikes. I hope that through my story others fall in love with this animal too, and that they in turn try their best to protect it.

Note: Strict regulations are in place for people swimming with whale sharks at Ningaloo Reef, and swimming with whale sharks for research purposes is managed through relevant permits and permissions.

Dr Sue Pillans is a marine scientist, artist and children's author and illustrator who specialises in creative and visual communications. Sue has always been drawn to nature and is passionate about sharing her deep love of the ocean through positive storytelling. Through her alter ego, Dr Suzie Starfish, she uses the art and science of storytelling to engage, excite, educate and empower children to be the change they want to 'sea' in the world.

Richard Pillans

Toni Jordan

Submersion

Now that my dominion is this house, this room, the topography of these four walls, I shut my eyes and think back to the memory of open water on my skin.

I am sitting on a floating platform in my bathers, rinsing the inside of my mask before fitting it tight and taking the snorkel in my mouth. The sun is fierce above me, but the ocean is crisp, and soon I will slide beneath the surface and every inch of me will feel alive. My hair will float like waving grass. I'm ungainly on my feet but here I'm buoyant, and a sturdy swimmer. A few dozen strokes will see me away from the boat, and then – a pivot, some strong kicks – I'm underneath the sea. I'm here for the feeling of suspension, but also for the fish. The clownfish, ridiculously orange, nestled in a sea anemone. The butterfly fish, striped and almost round, outlined with iridescent yellow. I hope for a turtle, if I'm lucky. The colours seem too vivid to be real. Every one of my senses knows that I am somewhere utterly foreign.

And there's one animal to thank for all this magnificence.

'The whole ecosystem is built by hard coral,' Dr Katharina Fabricius tells me. She's speaking from her home on Magnetic Island, off the coast of Townsville. 'We're used to the architecture of the land being constructed by plants, but not here. The reef is built by animals.'

I've spent the morning online, reading the work of some of Australia's most prominent marine researchers, and when I reach out to Katharina, a coral

Steve Smith

reef ecologist at the Australian Institute of Marine Science in Queensland, she's happy to chat. She explains that the entire Great Barrier Reef, which is about the size of Japan, was built by over 500 species of hard coral. These hardworking animals provide an ecosystem for around one million other species of animals and plants.

'Basically, they're soft-bodied animals with a hard skeleton, related to jellyfish. Their very thin tissue layer deposits their skeleton, and that's the hard substance that makes up the reef. They even record their environmental history in their skeleton in annual bands, almost like the way trees lay down layers of their trunks,' Katharina says. 'Some of them are small, only a few centimetres long. Others are many metres long and hundreds of years old. Together, corals form the habitat for the most diverse ecosystems in the marine world.'

And this ecosystem is built on symbiosis.

'The health of the reef is dependent on the capacity of species to live with each other in some kind of harmony,' Katharina says. Over the phone, her German accent makes me realise how far she's travelled, and how committed she is to the Great Barrier Reef. She's crossed the world. She's been a marine scientist since the late 1980s, but her voice is still full of wonder and passion for the coral she has been studying for decades.

Take the coral itself: tiny single-celled algae live within its tissues. These algae, being plants, photosynthesise. They pay 'rent' to their coral landlords in oxygen and sugars, which the coral then use to build their intricate cathedrals of calcium carbonate. And they're not immune to the effects of our changing climate.

'As the ocean becomes more acidic,' Katharina tells me, 'it becomes more difficult for the corals to form their skeletons from the carbonate in the water – and acidification is caused by the seawater absorbing carbon dioxide from the air. And this is on top of the stress of global warming. Right now, we're having a marine heatwave. The corals are bleaching in a similar way to 2016 and 2017, and it's not even an El Niño year.' Bleaching, Katharina says, is when the corals are so stressed that they expel the algae tenants from their tissues. 'Then, without the algae, they have no source of food or oxygen. They die of starvation,' she says.

It's a haunting image: all of those vivid colours, gone. Acres of bone-white coral skeletons, their dead fingers reaching towards the surface.

'We have more than just a fundamental moral responsibility to save the reef,' Katharina tells me. 'In Queensland alone, there are 66,000 jobs directly linked to tourism on the reef, and it brings in more than six billion dollars to the economy. All of that ends if the reef continues to die – the storm and erosion protection for the coast, the fisheries and the food they produce, the recreational uses, all of it.'

It's depressing that a marine scientist has to make an economic argument about the protection of a natural wonder, but here we are. The most pressing reason to save the reef, though, is almost impossible to quantify and invisible to the naked eye. We've all become very fond of breathing. Forget the Amazon being the lungs of the planet; around 50 per cent of the world's oxygen is made by the oceans. Yet corals are not cute and furry animals; they're squishy and almost gelatinous, with weird waving tentacles, like creatures from another planet. An individual coral polyp doesn't melt your heart the way an injured koala does. Amid the glory of the reef – the luminosity of the fish, the miracles of their own bony skeletons – the corals are easily overlooked by the recreational visitor. But if they fail, none of us can survive.

'It's the burning of fossil fuels that causes the increase in carbon dioxide in the air, which in turn leads to the acidification of the oceans,' Katharina says. 'We have to reduce our reliance on fossil fuels. It's that simple.'

From Magnetic Island, Katharina never loses sight of the marvel and spectacle of the ocean at her doorstep. She estimates she's spent over 2000 hours diving coral reefs around the world, so she's seen the changes in the world's reefs firsthand. Does she ever get sick of diving? The reef is her office, after all.

It takes her a moment to understand my question – it's such a ridiculous concept. 'Never,' Katharina finally says. 'I just love the diversity. The fish are so tame here; they come to you. It's like a different planet, yet it's a crucial part of our world. It's beautiful. It's like paradise, underwater.'

So often the natural world is only experienced through a screen or a window, but here on the reef, submersion means more than merely a physical descent. It's a memory that continues to sustain me now that we're living in the aquaria of our homes. I only hope the reef is still waiting for us when we emerge.

Toni Jordan is the author of five novels. The international bestseller *Addition* was longlisted for the Miles Franklin Literary Award, *Fall Girl* was published internationally, and *Nine Days* was awarded Best Fiction at the 2012 Indie Book Awards. *Our Tiny, Useless Hearts* (2016) was longlisted for the International Dublin Literary Award. Toni holds a Bachelor of Science in physiology and a PhD in creative arts. Her most recent novel is the literary mystery *The Fragments* (2018).

Cate Kennedy

Status: Near threatened

---

*Humanity's true moral test, its true test . . . consists of its attitude towards
those who are at its mercy: animals. And in this respect humankind has
suffered a fundamental debacle, a debacle so fundamental that all others
stem from it.*

—Milan Kundera, *The Unbearable Lightness of Being*

A few years back, the *Guardian Weekly* had a 'Notes and Queries' section
for readers that posed the question: 'At what point is a grouping of
humans considered civilised?' One respondent had said: 'When this question
does not need to be asked.'

Another had written: 'Gunpoint.' The first respondent came from New
Zealand. The man who had written 'Gunpoint' lived in Kenya.

Wouldn't it be nice if the question didn't need to be asked? Stand in front
of an animal in a cage for long enough, inside your human skin, and it will
soon become clear that there's no tranquil zen quip that will do here – the
question still needs to be asked again and again. At what point do we deem
ourselves civilised?

Many of us seek comfort by looking for ways to find a deeper and more
permanent engagement with wildlife and conservation. We try to push away
the dissonance, which asks us to hold in our minds simultaneously a kind of
irreconcilable battle about how we think the planet's faring, thanks to us. Are

Patrick Tomkins

I'm watching a small

rare animal sunning

itself, oblivious to me

in this moment.

I sit here, with my

never-ending grief

and never-ending

hunger, before this

tiny wild remnant of

a fragile world.

we at gunpoint, or can we go on believing the question doesn't need to be asked?

Several theories speculate that humans are the only primates to possess self-insight. Studies comparing sequences of aligned human and chimpanzee DNA first emerged in the 1970s. With the entire chimpanzee genome now mapped, it turns out we are, as the T-shirts tell us, 98 per cent chimp. It's the other 2 per cent that worries me – the percentage asserting that what separates us from all other animals is in fact the evolution of human morality, the capacity for altruism and sympathetic behaviour, based on the grasping of abstract notions of right and wrong and the common good.

So we watch, marvelling, as the primates at the zoo use their evolving opposable thumbs for climbing and fishing for termites with sticks, while we've used ours to weld cages together, wield machetes and chainsaws and test tubes, and squeeze a trigger.

When I was a child on school excursions to the Melbourne Zoo, I used to try to slip away from my classmates who travelled in squadrons with their worksheets. I would lurk in the Platypus House to watch the platypus swimming rapidly from one side of his murky pool to the other. The information board said the platypus was shy, and that seemed right – shy like an introverted kid at school was shy, getting the necessary contact over with as quickly as possible, racing for the private, lonely safety of a hiding place. A glimpse, then a trail of bubbles.

One day, forty years later, headed to the airport on my way to Queensland to teach a workshop, I took a detour and visited the enclosure again. It looked just the same, with a lone, shy platypus occasionally appearing in the brown water, hurrying from one side to another.

The next afternoon, outside Maleny in the Queensland hinterland, I went for a swim in an isolated river. I was sitting on the rocky bank, staring at the river in a bit of a trance, seeing small and subtle movements on the sunny surface of the water in front of me, before I realised what it was I was gazing at. A wild platypus. There was no hurry or shyness about this one; it played, ate and floated easily in the river, perfectly indifferent to me.

My first thought was: what are the odds of this? But as I sat smelling that clean river, listening to the birds and watching that platypus, what I felt was not jubilation or excitement, but a wave of sick, helpless grief. I'm 98 per cent chimp and 2 per cent other, so I'm a seething mass of contradictions. I want pristine places like this one declared World Heritage sites. I want to roll a giant boulder over the path that brought me to it, hiding, protecting and keeping it safe.

But safe from what? Safe from the same thing David Attenborough ruefully claimed is the greatest threat to biodiversity on the planet: too many mouths. Too many people just like me, who want to tramp in here with cameras, with backpacks, or with dirt bikes or mining licences, with cats and dogs and bulldozers and building permits, with a hankering for palm oil or rhino horn or rainforest timber, the seven billion of my own species. All of us with a terrible hunger. All of us with a ready narrative about why we deserve to get what we want.

What are the odds? Right here, in the middle of the full catastrophe, amid almost unprecedented mass extinction, the odds of a human alive today seeing a wild platypus are pretty much, close enough, seven billion to one. I sit spellbound by this wild river, full of pieties, full of demands, fed on my virtuous diet of ecological truisms, with a head full of nothing useful, just some bullshit bumper-sticker philosophy about touching the earth lightly. I'm watching a small rare animal sunning itself, oblivious to me in this moment. I sit here, with my never-ending grief and never-ending hunger, before this tiny wild remnant of a fragile world.

In front of me, the platypus rolls onto its back, and I see the glinting flash of its webbed hind leg. Then there's just a trail of bubbles, and it's gone.

Cate Kennedy is the author of the highly acclaimed novel *The World Beneath*, which won the People's Choice Award in the 2010 NSW Premier's Literary Awards. She is an award-winning short-story writer. Her two short-story collections, *Dark Roots* (Scribe, 2006) and *Like a House on Fire* (Scribe, 2012), are now both study texts on the Victorian school syllabus. *Dark Roots* was shortlisted for the Steele Rudd Award in the Queensland Premier's Literary Awards and for the Australian Literature Society Gold Medal. She is also the author of a travel memoir, *Sing, and Don't Cry*, and the poetry collections *Joyflight*, *Signs of Other Fires* and *The Taste of River Water*.

Ashley Hay

Owning the blue

_____

If I could be any creature, I've always thought I'd like to be a satin bowerbird, that Australian collector and scavenger, *Ptilonorhynchus violaceus*. I like the way it sounds as if it might have a hint of violet tucked inside its name.

I'd be a bowerbird because they embody a significant part of what I love about writing – the gathering, the collecting of bits of story and fact – and because of the pure power of the colour blue. Like the male satin bowerbird, I love this colour – the way it pulls me towards its surfaces, its depths. It's a colour I crave, a colour I love to possess.

I love how the bowerbirds amass and arrange so many things in so many tones of this one hue. Blue pegs, blue ribbons, blue bottle tops, blue straws, blue plastic, blue fabric – so much artificial blue. What would a bowerbird make of the colour of a butterfly's wing or a peacock's feather, the marine brilliance of a bluebottle, a blue button, a blue dragon?

In 2020, the Pantone Colour of the Year is 19-4052 Classic Blue: 'Instilling calm, confidence, and connection, this enduring blue hue highlights our desire for a dependable and stable foundation on which to build as we cross the threshold into a new era.'

Maybe – but blues have always felt to me more potentially active, more vivacious. More like Brett Whiteley's description of deep ultramarine, which he claimed had 'an obsessive, ecstasy-like effect upon my nervous system quite unlike any other colour'.

Steve Smith

Steve Smith

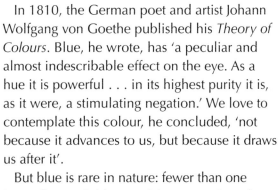

I spent a long time staring at those dragons' patterns, imagining the bite and gouging sizzle of their touch. I spent a long time envisaging their stinging potential as a rich, deep blue, just like their markings, wondering if they would smudge or stain my skin if I touched them.

In 1810, the German poet and artist Johann Wolfgang von Goethe published his *Theory of Colours*. Blue, he wrote, has 'a peculiar and almost indescribable effect on the eye. As a hue it is powerful . . . in its highest purity it is, as it were, a stimulating negation.' We love to contemplate this colour, he concluded, 'not because it advances to us, but because it draws us after it'.

But blue is rare in nature: fewer than one in ten flowers is blue, and the proportion of animals with naturally occurring blue features is lower again. Blue flowers generate their colour through a combination of red pigments – or anthocyanins – and reflected light. Think of delphiniums, bluebells, hydrangeas, cornflowers. The blue morpho butterfly gets its hue from structural colour – the fact that its wings bear microscopic scales that are ridged so as to reflect light a certain way. The iridescence of peacock feathers is reflected colour too, which comes from the viewing angle.

If the world appears to be at its bluest at the ocean's horizon, where water meets sky, it's along the shoreline that the purest and most vibrant of these chromas come into play: *Porpita porpita* (the blue button), *Physalia physalis* (the Portuguese man-of-war), *Physalia utriculus* (its smaller Australian relative, the bluebottle), and *Catostylus mosaicus* (the blue blubber jellyfish). These blues wash in from the deep.

'Everyone is asleep but the sea,' writes the poet Felicity Plunkett in 'Water Needles', 'knotting, un- / knotting the rope of its own approach.' Beneath this sense of perpetual exchange or conversation, blues come and go from the land's edge.

At New Brighton, on New South Wales'

northernmost shoreline, one late spring there was a pile of beached blue blubber jellyfish, dome after dome of translucent blue. They pulsed, as if they were still breathing.

They held a smorgasbord of different tones and textures: thick and rubbery on one side, grooved like a phonograph record underneath – I looked at them for a while and wondered what song those etched circles might play. Fish sing a dawn chorus: perhaps these creatures would too. The sea itself, beyond the shoreline, was vast and shiny, as if the surface had been sprinkled with sugar. It glittered in spots; it glistened and shone. Blue blubbers are the most commonly encountered jellyfish along Australia's eastern coastline – I found a stick, returned one to the sea, and told myself that that had made a difference.

The next day there were dozens more washed up and stranded.

Their colours – the deepest of which sit between peacock blue and dark teal – are, according to marine biologist Lisa-ann Gershwin, 'common in animals that live at the air–water interface . . . thought to protect them from UV damage and possibly aid in camouflage'. These hues have shorter wavelengths and higher frequencies in the visible colour spectrum.

Perhaps that's what drives the sense of life inside these colours. Blue, said French artist Yves Klein, is 'the invisible becoming visible'. He patented his own luminous International Klein Blue, suspending its pigment in a synthetic primer that would hold more of the colour intact. And sometimes that luminosity comes out of the ocean – from invisible to visible – and settles in a Morse code of dots and dashes of perfect blue.

Glaucus atlanticus, a small sea slug, or nudibranch, is its own carnival of colours, stripes and starburst shapes. A distinct silver-blue mollusc with three sets of arms, it has many common names – the sea swallow, the blue angel, the dragon slug and the blue dragon – like a poem all its own.

The blue dragon was first named in 1705 by the German-Polish zoologist and entomologist Johann Philipp Breyne, who mistook it for a leech. It was more correctly scooped into the taxonomic catalogue as a marine mollusc over seventy years later by Johann Forster, the young naturalist who accompanied Captain James Cook on his second vast voyage through the Pacific.

On Stradbroke Island last summer, one degree of latitude above my earlier blue blubber jellyfish site, small stripes of these spiky flares glowed blue along the shore. As walls of smoke rose from the west, it felt as if the whole edge of Australia was on fire, but here there was only blue water and sky.

My son, aged eleven, leant forward to touch a blue dragon with a stick: a friend of his, he said, had done a project about them – which oceans they lived in, the power of their sting. The coolest thing, he told me, was that they feasted on bluebottles, including the Portuguese man-of-war. They ate those bluebottles' poison and stored it for their own use. I'm reading descriptions of this process now: how they can eat a whole creature and select the stinging cells – the venomous nematocysts – to store and deploy later on.

But there's no guarantee they'll sting you, my son told me. Whereas their prey, those man-of-war bluebottles, can't help themselves, the blue dragons may sting you, or they may not.

I stood there for a long time, thinking about the discretionary use of accumulated power. I spent a long time staring at those dragons' patterns, imagining the bite and gouging sizzle of their touch. I spent a long time envisaging their stinging potential as a rich, deep blue, just like their markings, wondering if they would smudge or stain my skin if I touched them.

It would be something, I thought, to collect that blue for a cyanophilic bower – and I let my finger trace the outline of a dragon's shape, above its threat.

I felt the edge of an idea beginning to form, drawing me after it, like Goethe's definition of blue. There's something in the notion of storing and sharing power somehow, like the storing and sharing of knowledge.

The damage we've done, scooping things up, appropriating and exploiting, imposing ourselves and our desires on other ecologies, when we need to imagine a different – more integrated – kind of cohabitation, see ourselves as part of everything else.

On the beach, at my feet, these bright small things shimmered, circus-stripes crossed with weapons, marks of brilliant blue beneath the wide span of the sky.

Ashley Hay, a novelist, is the editor of *Griffith Review*. Her novels have been published in Australia, the UK, the US and in translation; *The Railwayman's Wife* won the 2013 Colin Roderick Award and the People's Choice Award at the 2014 NSW Premier's Literary Awards. Her work has also been awarded the Bragg UNSW Press Prize for Science Writing. Her most recent novel is *A Hundred Small Lessons*.

Tracy Sorensen

Symbiosis

My mother was wearing a purple bikini as she waded into the water of Coral Bay. She was slender, and you could see the vertebrae in a line down her back. She was very short-sighted. Sometimes we'd make her take her glasses off and describe what she could and could not see. Her hands were clear in front of her face but further away became blurred, and beyond that just looked like blobs and shapes – a fanning watercolour. For snorkelling, she unscrewed the arms from an old pair of glasses and stuck the lenses onto her face mask with sticky tape. When she put her face into the water, a school of tiny blue fish sprang sharply into view.

She thought the water was crystal clear, kissed by glittering sunlight. There was the fresh world, blue out towards India, and in the other direction the white sand of the bay and the pinkish dunes with silvery tufts of vegetation on top. The world was giant, clean, uninhabited.

Except that it wasn't. Every drop of water touching her skin, wetting her long brown hair, was teeming with ten million unseen viruses. And all of the land, all of the sea, was thick with the unheard stories of other people.

I had my own face mask, snorkel and flippers. I, too, saw the bright-blue fish. I only had to walk into the water, kick up my legs and float facedown, breathing loudly past my own ears.

Afterwards, Mum fed a driftwood fire and fried fish in a blackened pan. We ate the ordinary fish, probably bream, not the pretty little ones. There were

Justin Bruhn

always bones to worry about. They'd hide themselves in the cooked white flesh, unmoored from their spines, ready to stick you in the back of the throat.

I mostly knew coral as a dead thing, bits of white broken staghorn, pitted like the face of a young man who'd had acne. It was sometimes dyed to replicate the colours of the reef, stuck with glue to vases or clamshells to make ornaments. Mrs Boon, just down the road from us, used to paint seascapes in oils on the inner surface of giant fluted clamshells. One day, unexpectedly, she let us play with her paints, squeezing a little colour out of the tubes, giving each child a paintbrush. But the colours quickly blended into an unsatisfying grey.

There's a virus, but this one is not benign. Mum goes into lockdown in her small wing at the back of my sister's house, on the Central Coast of New South Wales. She listens for noises in the house, her grandchildren playing or shouting at each other. The sound of a car starting, a pot clattering. Food is passed to her, and rolls of toilet paper. She has the television on, with subtitles for the hard of hearing. She is keeping safe.

My mother swims over the coral, shedding tiny quantities of calcium from hair and skin and nails. These molecules, no longer hers, float in the sea water at Coral Bay. They're sucked in through the fingers of a coral polyp, taken deep into its own calcifying space where they will be converted to limestone.

She has a few shells in her small bookcase, but most of the collection is at my place in Bathurst, where there's more room: clamshells, a big bailer shell, cowries, cat's eyes, conches, angel wings. We took what we wanted.

'She has duck's disease,' says Dad. I look at Mum, standing at the sink, washing the dishes. What is duck's disease? 'Her bum is too close to the ground,' he says affectionately. I'm still not getting it. 'She's *short*,' says Dad, spelling it out. To me, small for my age, Mum is tall and slender. She sews herself red hotpants out of a fabric called crimplene. She is proud of her flat stomach. She is nothing like a duck.

We all feed from the sea that washes against the land at Carnarvon, where we live. We eat prawns that come in off the trawlers, crayfish that Dad simply lifts out of their hiding places in the reefs at the blowholes, Warroora or Coral

Bay. The cats know when we're going fishing – they can smell the rods and hand reels as we get them out of the shed – and wait eagerly for fresh kill. The galah, who lives in a small cage on the cracked concrete between the back door and the outdoor toilet, might get a cuttlebone that we have picked up off the beach. She sinks her beak into the soft white substance. She closes her eyes in pleasure. It's like the pleasure we get from peeling the skin from each other's sunburned backs, a few days later, when they start to itch and prickle.

I'm in lockdown, too. And landlocked, unable to get to the coast. The Pacific is not the Indian Ocean, but waves still crash on rocks and there's that slick gleam on the sand at the water's edge. There's foam and spray. Now that I'm not allowed to go, it's all I want. I call up Google Earth and fly along the coast over Carnarvon, the blowholes, Warroora and Coral Bay. I zoom parallel to the earth, collapsing time, moving backwards and forwards. There is the turquoise sea, the shelves of reef, the red earth, the sparse paint-blobs of acacia bush. It's a God's-eye view, a diabolical view from nowhere, a view my eyes were not evolved to see.

We are becalmed, in the doldrums.

Overwhelmed by drought, bushfires and COVID-19, this year's coral bleaching barely makes the news.

Warmer water has made the coral polyps go crazy, spitting out the tiny organisms that help nourish them and give them their colours. There's a flash, a fluorescence, and the zooxanthellae are gone, rendering the polyps see-through against their white skeletons.

My mother swims over the coral, shedding tiny quantities of calcium from hair and skin and nails. These molecules, no longer hers, float in the sea water at Coral Bay. They're sucked in through the fingers of a coral polyp, taken deep into its own calcifying space where they will be converted to limestone. She's swimming, she's watching fish and she's sharing some tiny part of herself with the coral.

124

Tracy Sorensen grew up in Carnarvon, a remote town on the north coast of Western Australia, and now lives in Bathurst, New South Wales. Her debut novel, *The Lucky Galah*, published by Picador in 2018, was longlisted for the 2019 Miles Franklin Literary Award. She is currently the 2020 Writer in Residence at Sydney University's Charles Perkins Centre, and is a PhD candidate researching climate change communication at Charles Sturt University.

Tony Birch

Salt.Fresh.Water.Sea

The contemporary mouth of the Birrarung River flows into a young bay (in terms of deep time). Prior to the Ice Age the waterway known by Europeans as Port Phillip Bay was open country belonging to the Kulin nation. The bay was formed as a result of the ending of the Ice Age, with water filling grasslands over an extended period between approximately 13,000 and 8000 years ago. Today, the Birrarung meets not only the bay, but the Maribyrnong River, which weaves its way through the volcanic country of Melbourne's west.

Since the British invasion in the early nineteenth century, the Kulin waterways, both fresh and saltwater, have been damaged, desecrated and manipulated to serve the interests of colonial and capital expansion. This has come at great cost to country, people and non-human species. We should not require a brave seventeen-year-old girl from Sweden to tell us that we are killing the planet, but with the exception of Indigenous peoples across the globe and committed environmental activists, the communal deafness to warnings passionately articulated by young climate warriors such as Greta Thunberg is staggeringly negligent.

Too many of us, individually and collectively, suffer an absence of humility with regard to our relationship to the planet. Rather than consider, as Indigenous societies understand inherently, that we should live in partnership with the planet and, when necessary, defer to its authority, we have repeatedly attempted to *conquer* the natural environment in a one-sided

Patrick Tomkins

war that has raged far, far longer than any conflict between human societies. What we fail to realise is that, while many species and ecologies have been destroyed and lost for all time, we are also on a pathway to the destruction of human society if we do not alter the way we live *with* the planet. The planet itself will survive for some time and, as it managed to do in the past, will eventually adapt to challenging circumstances. Fortunately, or not, there will be no coming back for us. Unless. Unless we genuinely change our relationship to country.

If you were to stand on the bank of the Birrarung River, at its mouth, you would be in the presence of deep Indigenous time. Below the surface of the water the riverbed of the older river, the pre-Ice Age river, would be waiting for you. The old riverbed is there, and it snakes its way across the bay where it eventually meets the ocean. At this point the old riverbed lies one hundred metres down in a crevice just outside Port Phillip Heads. The relatively young bay was formed slowly, patiently, over many thousands of years when the relationships between human societies, non-human species and water – fresh and salt – were based on mutual respect and reciprocity. Think about the ancient Birrarung and consider the extent to which the arrogance of imperial-capitalist societies have not only acted with neglect towards country, but with wanton stupidity.

Standing on the bank of the Birrarung River, please also consider this. It is at this location that salt and fresh water meet; that the ocean water enters the bay and meets the fresh water of two mighty river systems that have given life, and existed *with* life, for tens of thousands of years. Many Aboriginal people across Australia identify as either 'saltwater' or 'freshwater' people, depending on their nation's relationship to water. It is inspiring to consider that the meeting of fresh and salt water in the heartland of industrial Melbourne produces both a metaphor and reality for Aboriginal sustenance and inter-nation connections.

While standing on the bank of the Birrarung, also imagine a couple of facts that should encourage us to search ourselves thoroughly until we do discover and welcome the humility we require to survive. Think of the oceans and imagine something like a cubic metre of salt water, around the amount it takes to fill a decent bathtub. Imagine that cubic metre of salt water moving through oceans, intermingling with plant and animal species as it travels. Its journey will be long and, again, require patience. That cubic metre of water will eventually circumnavigate the globe. The journey will take around one thousand years. That is one thousand years for every cubic metre in the world's oceans today, out there now, moving, shifting and engaging.

Now imagine the vital molecules that share life with fresh water, in our rivers, creeks and lakes. Water molecules are tough. They are persistent. You may have heard of 'slow TV' or the 'slow food' movement. Well, a water molecule that decides to take a rest in fresh groundwater can wait for up to ten thousand years before deciding to move on and live. We could call this 'slow living'. At the confluence of the Birrarung River and Port Phillip Bay, a story, a meeting many thousands of years in the making, has been occurring for many more thousands of years, and is occurring now.

Imagine this as you stand under a bridge transporting thousands of people in thousands of cars and trucks, on a daily basis, always in a rush. Under the bridge, the meeting of salt and fresh water is constantly under threat from pollution, dredges, the dumping of human waste, and sheer ignorance. Somewhere, perhaps in the Arctic Circle, water is gathering again. It will begin a journey along a conveyor belt supplied by the ocean's currents. Meanwhile, on the bed of the old river, one hundred metres below the bay perhaps, fresh water molecules are sleeping. At some point in the future, perhaps tomorrow, or possibly one thousand years from now, more fresh and salt water will meet.

Do not forget this. Please. And also, remember this. That bathtub full of water about to leave the Arctic? It will begin yet another epic journey for you and me, for all species, human and non-human. One cubic metre is about to shift to enable our survival. Finally, please consider the following. Are we so negligent and thoughtless that we are prepared to deny a courageous journey that will allow salt and sea water to meet and thrive?

Tony Birch is the author of three novels: the bestselling *The White Girl*, winner of the 2020 NSW Premier's Indigenous Writers' Prize; *Ghost River*, winner of the 2016 Victorian Premier's Literary Award for Indigenous Writing; and *Blood*, which was shortlisted for the Miles Franklin Literary Award. He is also the author of *Shadowboxing* and three short story collections, *Father's Day*, *The Promise* and *Common People*. In 2017 he was awarded the Patrick White Literary Award. Tony is a frequent contributor to ABC local and national radio, a regular guest at writers' festivals, and a climate justice campaigner. He lives in Melbourne.

Air

Georgina Steytler

Holly Ringland

Torn love letters:
How butterflies instruct a life

In 2019, I was invited to the launch of the French publication of my debut novel. So, one summer afternoon, there I was, in Paris, at a mint-green table outside La Maison Rose, the pastel-pink house on a narrow cobblestone street that has been serving coffee for over one hundred years. (I later learnt it was also a favourite haunt of Picasso, and was once a boarding house where local writers could get inexpensive meals.) While I waited for my glass of rosé and *salade niçoise*, I was absorbed by Montmartre in the headiness of June. Couples sauntered by with arms linked; a gaggle of teenagers swung around streetlight poles, alternately smoking thin cigarettes and sucking lollipops; a red-lipped woman opened a latched window in an ivy-covered stone house overlooking the Rue de l'Abreuvoir, where I sat, to yell a torrent of French at someone below. When my wine arrived, I reached a hand forward to take a sip and noticed that La Maison Rose's pink walls and green shutters matched the colours in the native Australian flowers and butterflies I'd recently had tattooed on my right forearm.

An acute sense of gratitude went through me; how slim the odds of that moment were, that I'd ever sit at a century-old writers' house on a cobbled street in Paris, all because I'd written my first novel. It took a determined act of personal transformation that began with scraping together enough courage to believe in the possibility of another future for my life. I'd reached down into myself and found the will to resist and subvert violence and trauma and

Nick Monaghan

to believe in my own worth. My own dreams. The wave of emotion I felt at that moment brought to mind a quote from one of my favourite writers, Alice Hoffman:

> Some things, when they change, never do return to the way
> they once were.
> Butterflies, for instance, and women who've been in love
> with the wrong man too often.

I'd held those words close like a prayer for more than a decade. They reminded me of the exquisite, mysterious beauty that can come from trusting in transformation. They also offered a layered, difficult certainty: how merciless the finality of loss can be, and at the same time, the unexpected magic that loss can yield.

Two truths: I've always loved butterflies, and I've lived with complex trauma as a result of male-perpetrated violence for much of my life. In 2009, I used my life savings to make my first migration from my homeland, Australia, to Europe. I was desperate to claw my way into a new version of myself, after finding the will to leave what would be the last violent relationship in my life. To Paris I went, with a bag, a tent, my oldest friend, and a notebook with Alice Hoffman's words and a lemon migrant butterfly wing pressed inside; I'd found the wing on my front doorstep the morning I left Australia.

The city of light left me slack-jawed with wonder and fatigued by unresolved trauma. Life felt precarious back then, manageable only moment by moment. Each night, in my tent by the Seine, I wrote in my notebook everything I'd felt that day. Before sleeping, I'd flick to the page where the lemon migrant wing was pressed, and I read Alice Hoffman's words over and again, asking myself to be brave enough to forge ahead, not go backwards. Asking myself to welcome transformation. That papery, pale-yellow wing, which over time turned to dust between the pages, reminded me it was possible to go through periods of great darkness and still emerge to fly. It's the same metaphor that has kept humans enchanted with butterflies throughout history.

Butterflies are estimated to have evolved 80 to 120 million years ago. Some of the most well-known myths featuring the butterfly come from ancient Egypt, where people believed that butterflies carried the souls of the dead. Butterflies were depicted on Egyptian tombs and gravestones as long as 2500 years ago. Lesser-known yet older butterfly stories are told in Australian Aboriginal culture: Mununja the Butterfly is a Ngunawal Dreamtime story

The autumn air is

thick with wild lemon

migrant butterflies.

They remind me that,

despite everything,

transformation is still

possible. It may be

unfathomable. And yet,

it is still truth. We can

change ourselves for

the better.

that has been shared for thousands of years, passed from generation to generation. As told by Ngunawal Elder Don Bell, Mununja was a young Aboriginal girl who transformed into a butterfly to avoid marrying the wicked and powerful Gunga. He would always prevent her from marrying the boy she loved, but with the help of the good spirit butterfly Naja, Mununja was able to stay near her family and her country forever, as a beautiful butterfly.

If I could go back to those nights by the Seine, I would write Mununja the Butterfly's story in my notebook next to Alice Hoffman's quote, to remind myself how fear, resistance and escape can sometimes transform a life for the better.

I grew up in subtropical South East Queensland, on Bundjalung country, between the pages of my books and the plants and trees in the gardens of the women who loved me. Like many children, my imagination was captured early by butterflies: blue triangles, lemon migrants, monarchs, blue tigers. My first sense of the power of what butterflies have to teach us about ourselves came from reading Eric Carle's classic, *The Very Hungry Caterpillar*, in which a caterpillar goes through its life cycle to eventually transform into a butterfly. That such a profound change was possible and wasn't a fictitious conjuring from one of my fairytales made me realise that magic was real in the world. It was in nature. As a result, I've sought butterflies throughout my life, for what they tell us about the beauty to be found in impermanence, and how change, even if unwanted, can awaken our own innate acts of transformation. As Victor Hugo wrote of pain, transformed:

> . . . torn love-letters, that through the skies
> Flutter, and float, and change to butterflies.

In my mid-thirties, after I finished writing the draft of my first novel, I got my first tattoo on my right arm: a lemon migrant butterfly at my wrist becomes a woman, who rises to become a monarch butterfly. *Some things, when*

134

they change, never do return to the way they once were. It's a truth I think of now every time I see butterflies in the wild, or glance at my transformed skin. Loss, change, hope. Beauty. Nature is our great teacher: like butterflies, we are born to evolve, transform and emerge. I wear butterflies on my body to ponder the ages of my life: what magic might be possible if we allow ourselves to be exactly who we are? What kind of transformation might happen if we find the courage to allow pain to change us, and accept this by trusting in ourselves?

I'm writing this on Yugambeh country, in my Queensland garden, a long way from a tent on the Seine. A long way from the trauma I once needed to ask myself not to return to. Those prayers are torn love letters now.

The autumn air is thick with wild lemon migrant butterflies. They remind me that, despite everything, transformation is still possible. It may be unfathomable. And yet, it is still truth. We can change ourselves for the better.

It's the magic in us.

It's in our nature.

Holly Ringland's debut novel, *The Lost Flowers of Alice Hart*, was published in 2018 and became an international bestseller, translated into twenty-seven languages. In 2019 it won the ABIA General Fiction Book of the Year, and it is currently being adapted for television by Bruna Papandrea's Made Up Stories. In 2020, Holly began filming *Back to Nature*, a visually stunning eight-episode ABC series that she is co-hosting with Aaron Pedersen. Holly's second novel, *The Seven Skins of Esther Wilding*, will be published by HarperCollins in 2022.

Nick Monaghan

Kirli Saunders

Garrall

At school
on a cloudy Tuesday
Aunty Lindy
   sits our class in a circle
   by the lake.
Facing inwards
   she talks about respect
   in a space like this –
about the timelessness
   of our meeting,
and the importance of caring for
   the Country that you sit on,
   and the Country you belong to.
Aunty Lindy explains
   listening deeply
   means hearing from the heart:
   hearing with more
   than ears.
She tells us
   of garrall,
   a budjan

Matt Wright

Andrew Buckle

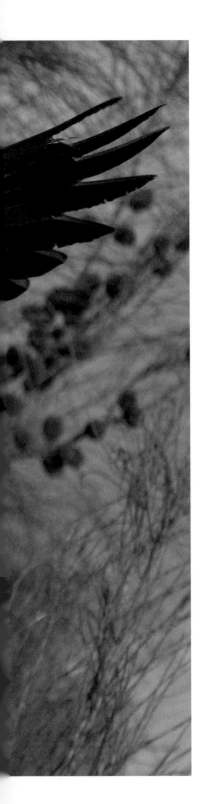

with symbolic colours –
  black, red and yellow,
her Duwi,
  sacred to our nation –
  a totem budjan,
  one that sings in the karrat
  and speaks of canbe.
We pause to hear her calls
  from far away:
naora
naora
naora
Hands to daore,
  we join Aunty
  planting she-oaks.
We palm their seed pods,
  rough and symmetrical.
  She says that they
  will keep us safe,
  and connect us to the Old People.

We drip water
  at the base
  of trunks to be.
We erect small sentries
  to protect the seedlings.
I hope they will
  withstand the drought,
and welcome the budjan,
  and their karrat.

——Kirli Saunders, 'Garrall', from *Bindi*
(Magabala Books)

140

Like the main character of this verse novel, *Bindi*, I was born on Gundungurra Country, and blessed with abundant adventures in the bawa – where lessons of firm respect and deep adoration for our Gummuang Daoure were instilled in us as goodjahgah. I remember watching budjan-wulali come and go as witnesses, and messengers. I remember the magpies, gang gangs, lyrebirds and bowerbirds, but especially, I recall the heart-stopping black-cockatoos with their red tails and ancestral calls.

Garrall, the glossy black-cockatoo, is nearly fifty centimetres in length. Painted brownish-black, it has a small crest. Males have bright-red tail panels, and females a wider reddish-yellow tail, barred with black. They also have gold-flecked cheeks.

Culturally, garrall is a spirit bird, who sings in the rain and speaks of the fire. There are many Dreaming stories about her across the continent. The glossy black-cockatoo nests in the hollows of trees that are older than us all, and feeds only on the casuarinas of woodlands or timbered watercourses.

Since colonisation, threats to garralls include the destruction of habitat due to farming and clearing, and the impacts of bushfires. The glossy black-cockatoo is also threatened by feral cats and possums that raid nests, galahs, and introduced honey bees who share limited nesting trees.

On Gundungurra Country and across New South Wales, the glossy black-cockatoo is listed as vulnerable, and if action is not taken, garrall, and her significance for our people, will become endangered across the state. She is already regionally extinct in parts of western Victoria and south-eastern South Australia.

In recent years I've been teaching and learning the Gundungurra language alongside Elders Aunty Val Mulcahy and Aunty Sharyn Halls, and Custodian Aunty Trish Levett, with Red Room Poetry, for my Poetry in First Languages (PIFL) project.

PIFL celebrates, shares and preserves knowledge of First Nations languages and culture through the arts. It engages First Nations students in cultural and art workshops

It gives me hope that one day, my own goodjahgah will plant our much-needed trees, that they'll greet the garrall in Gundungurra as they move through the bawa with custodial care – hope that our spirit bird's ancestral calls will always be there.

Andrew Buckle

Andrew Buckle

delivered on Country, by community, supporting our young people to conserve our languages and landscapes.

On Gundungurra Country, we've been grateful to deliver PIFL alongside Wingecarribee Shire Council and the Department of Planning, Industry and Environment's Glossies in the Mist team, part of the Saving our Species program. This has meant that our students have been able to learn about the garrall and the significance of the casuarina and her Duwi seeds, and have been supported to plant trees and write poems to honour them.

Students' poems about the garrall and her habitat, in the Gundungurra language, have been published on the Red Room Poetry website, and we've watched their beautiful words fly around the shire on the backs of buses, in a collaboration with Bundjalung artist David Cragg.

This process has been heartwarming, and the growing awareness among the broader community of the impacts of habitat removal, and the need to conserve both the land and our language, has been reassuring.

The highlight, though, has been watching our next generation of Elders learn the names of our plants and animals in the Gundungurra language, and seeing them press their hands to Gummuang Daoure as they raise the seedlings of Duwi trees.

It gives me hope that one day, my own goodjahgah will plant our much-needed trees, that they'll greet the garrall in Gundungurra as they move through the bawa with custodial care – hope that our spirit bird's ancestral calls will always be there.

Kirli Saunders is a proud Gunai woman and an award-winning international children's author and poet, as well as a teacher and emerging artist. She leads the Poetry in First Languages project, delivered by Red Room Poetry. Her debut picture book, *The Incredible Freedom Machines*, was shortlisted for the Prime Minister's Literary Awards and CBCA Notables. Her poetry collection, *Kindred*, was shortlisted for the 2020 ABIAs and Booktopia's Favourite Australian Book (FAB) Award. She is the inaugural winner of the Daisy Utemorrah Award and the University of Canberra's Aboriginal and Torres Strait Islander Poetry Prize (2019). Kirli is an esteemed judge for the Val Vallis Award and the Prime Minister's Literary Awards, and is the 2020 NSW Aboriginal Woman of the Year.

144

Anne
Buist

The birds

The black monsters are watching and waiting, lined up on the powerline that stretches across the paddock fifty metres away.

Do crows eat wrens, I wonder? I sit watching from my verandah; a tiny, brilliant-blue bird flies between the wires around the balcony, playing hide-and-seek with its plain brown girlfriend. I glare at the black monsters in the distance; they must be twenty times the weight of my little friends.

The crows have checked me out and decided it's worth the risk. Eight swoop in closer, taking up positions in the fruit trees. At least they show no interest in the hard green nuggets, no bigger than walnuts, that will never get to be full-sized apples. The rosellas, in all their green and red glory, come for the fruit, but they don't arrive until early evening; someone else's orchard must be doing appetisers. I don't mind the rosellas having the apples; the trees are old and gnarled and covered in moss, more history than promise. I resent the loss of the cherries more, but we let the tree grow too large to reach the top branches without a cherry picker, which wouldn't fit in the yard anyway. I think of it as live television. In town I'd be watching the news at six pm. Here I watch the rosellas.

Now the black monsters – Alfred Hitchcock has a lot to answer for (I'm not big on seagulls either) – come closer. Orderly, like they've taken a number, are waiting their turn. The alpha bird flies to the edge of the birdbath, stares me down, then jumps in. There is so much splashing I wonder if there'll be

Georgina Steytler

Georgina Steytler

As I watch these birds, I feel intensely protective. Motherly. What will happen to them if it burns here? How can I save them? I feel visceral pain in the knowledge that I can't.

any water left for bird number two, let alone number eight.

I'm not the only one wondering. There's a change in proceedings today. A solo magpie swoops in. The unwashed black monsters go running. The clean one flies off. The magpie seems to be grinning at me as it jumps the queue, drinks and cools itself in the shade of the cherry tree. I thank my black and white friend and, when the bird's done, I head down to refill the bath. Before the rosellas arrive there will be ten or so wrens who will play here. Of all the locals, these are perhaps my favourite, though I wish the kookaburras would come down from the far gum tree where they sing the evening serenade. They and the screeching cockatoos (not to be encouraged, as when they used to visit they chewed all the wood around our windows) must use the water in the dam; our one is low, but there is still some moisture over the mud and silt.

This is my twice-daily weekend ritual. More relaxing than yoga or mindfulness. The dizzy beauty of nature right before my eyes. My bird book in hand as I try to identify the more unusual visitors.

This year it was different.

Different because the rest of the state is burning – man-made climate change has transformed the usual fires into catastrophic ones – and as I watch these birds, I feel intensely protective. Motherly. What will happen to them if it burns here? How can I save them? I feel visceral pain in the knowledge that I can't. That planting native trees with bird- and bee-attracting flowers, fighting the rabbits and drought to get the birds established, and refilling the birdbath will

148

count for naught against a wall of flame.

Different this year also because the previous October I walked a thousand kilometres across the French–Italian Alps, and stood in an Italian forest and listened to deathly silence. *Silent Spring*. Yes, this was European autumn, but with climate change it feels at times as if Armageddon is coming; was it happening here before my eyes, caused by loss of habitat, the use of chemicals in farm management, and too many birds hunted for Italian mammas' pots?

Despite the distant bushfires, the black monsters arrive as usual. I open my bird book and finally realise they aren't crows or ravens – they're choughs; better still, a chatter of choughs. I look at their orange-red eyes, the flash of white underneath, and wonder how I hadn't noticed.

This year I welcome my choughs. They aren't monsters at all. Unlike humans, it seems they live in harmony with their environment. They take their turn – and they let the wrens take theirs.

Anne Buist is Chair of Women's Mental Health at the University of Melbourne and has thirty years of clinical and research experience in perinatal psychiatry, including forensic work. She is the author of a trilogy with a tart-noir heroine, psychiatrist Natalie King, and a standalone rural novel, *The Long Shadow*. She has been married to Graeme Simsion for thirty years, and together they have written a feel-good midlife novel, *Two Steps Forward*, with a sequel in progress.

Georgina Steytler

Barbara Allen

The scoop

A scoop of sugar, a scoop of ice cream? Sure. But a scoop of pelicans? What a quirky collective noun for this magnificent bird. It sits alongside other odd collective nouns for pelicans: a brief, a pod, a pouch, a squadron. How, I wonder, did any of these terms come to describe the beautiful birds taking off from the water in front of me?

A *squadron* fits the image of a group of these birds in formation, gracefully gliding across the sky. A *pod* is the term used for the care of their young. Pelicans, like humans, cluster their young together, in creches or pods, guarded by several adults. A huge *pouch* is what we are drawn to when spotting a pelican, an avian Santa with a bulging sack hanging from its bill. A *brief* doesn't really fit, unless you are a fan of John Grisham's novels, but a scoop? Could this be a large-enough term to honour these avian marvels who reside within the Australian psyche, who with bold wing-strokes outline the Australian coastline and its inland lakes and channels?

No, *scoop* is too small a word, too commonplace a utensil to describe a group of pelicans. Unless, perhaps, the scoop serves as an icon? By virtue of its hollow structure, a scoop leaves room for something, becomes a vessel to be filled. Pelicans are both icons – in that they point beyond themselves to the sacred – and iconic – in that they are widely recognised. *Icon* is a religious term, and there is something of the hallowed about the pelican. They inhabit cathedrals and churches, are found masterfully carved on choir stalls,

Wayne Suffield

are embroidered on altar cloths and embossed on silver chalices. They have become a symbol for Christ, due to a legend which says that, during times of drought, the pelican would pluck its breast and feed its young on its own blood, sometimes dying in the process. It is not hard to see why the pelican has been appropriated by the church.

What do we make of our Australian pelican, one of eight species worldwide, its huge squat body caricatured, its shovel-like pouch lampooned? Pelicans resemble flying dinosaurs, which is fitting because birds are descendants of theropods. Incomplete fossils from the early Cretaceous period have unearthed a pelican-like pterosaur. Of ancient lineage, the pelican is our elder. One Indigenous tale depicts the pelican as the giver of two gifts to humans: opals and fire. In another, its spacious pouch hides fishing nets, and when this is discovered, the pelican, named Gulayaali (which means 'two nets' in the language of the Gamilaraay people of northern New South Wales), teaches humans how to make nets for fishing. In a cautionary tale, however, the pelicans' black plumage is a visible reminder of their having broken tribal law, violating a taboo, and therefore suffering retribution.

What taboos do we humans break, transgress, when we build on these birds' habitat and nesting sites, taint the waterways, kill them with plastic waste, and injure them with fishing tackle and hooks?

We cannot domesticate the pelican, even though we may dream of doing so. *Storm Boy*, the famous book by Colin Thiele, is a misnamed story. Its proper title should have been *Mr Percival*, because it was the Australian

What does the 'spectacled pelican' see when it fixes me with its steely gaze? Kin? A featherless friend? Or a destroyer of its habitat?

Wayne Suffield

Wayne Suffield

pelican who charmed us, won our hearts, made us wish he was our very own. But that can never be, because the pelican is wild, untameable, stitched to the seascape, and will not sit sedately at our hearths.

When I read *Storm Boy* as a child, I felt for the boy, but I wept for Mr Percival, and willed him to live. I learnt then that not all stories have happy endings. As an adult, I felt a mother's love for Storm Boy. I wanted to wrap him in my arms, cuddle the grieving child who would never be the same, because the death of a loved one is a step closer to adulthood. I may have cried for the boy's loss, but I wept more for Mr Percival, my tears a wet litany for all suffering creatures.

The Australian pelican, *Pelecanus conspicillatus*, is also known as the spectacled pelican, because of the ring of bare skin around its eyes. The Latin *conspicio* means to 'look carefully', and *conspicillum* 'a place to look from'. Dutch naturalist Coenraad Temminck called the bird *Pélican á lunettes*, as it is still known in French – and in German, *Brillenpelikan* ('spectacled pelican'). What does the 'spectacled pelican' see when it fixes me with its steely gaze? Kin? A featherless friend? Or a destroyer of its habitat?

Does it sense my awe and love for the biological marvel that it is? The Australian pelican holds two Guinness World Records, one for the length of its bill (the longest in the avian world), and the other for its longevity (Percy, an Australian pelican, lived at the Wellington Zoo for sixty-two years). It is an anatomical and genetic wonder.

At the beginning of the day, watching the sun rise over the ocean, I long to see these squadrons of the skies. If we are not careful, the legend of the pelican plucking its breast to feed its young may become a reality. As an icon, the pelican points towards the preservation of life, the protection of wildness, both externally and in our souls. The pelican's broad wingspans bridge the sacred and the secular, a sun-drenched icon, touched by the holy, radiant.

I turn away from the scoop, now transformed into a dazzling blaze, beaten gold by the rising sun. As I move towards home, the icon's image travels with me, encased, protected within my heart.

Reverend Barbara Allen is a minister in the Uniting Church in Australia. She has had several books published: *I Was There* (St Paul's Press, 2009), *Pigeon* (Reaktion Books, 2009), *Animals in Religion* (Reaktion Books, 2016) and *Pelican* (Reaktion Books, 2019). She was the first chaplain at the Lort Smith Animal Hospital, Melbourne.

Jack
Pascoe

Living for country:
What else is there to live for?

I was born in Carlton, but I was grown on Cape Otway. Many of my first
memories involve eating rice out of the billy, cooked on a fire next to our
caravan directly adjacent to the building site that would become my family
home.

I still eat rice, albeit reluctantly, if it's the type of overcooked slurry that
normally comes out of a billy. But the place, the place never leaves me, and
I wonder if I can ever leave the place.

It was named, in that casually insulting manner adopted by colonisers, after
Captain William Albany Otway of the Royal British Navy by his dear friend
and the Cape's 'discoverer' Lieutenant James Grant. Otway, predictably,
never took the time to visit. A poor name then.

But the place never forgot its story, or its true name, or its people.

I left the Cape to study but returned frequently until my parents moved so
that Dad could live on country. We are both Yuin men and our traditional
lands stretch across the south coast of New South Wales and dip into the
northern coastal areas of Victoria, far from the Otway Range. But when my
university finally entrusted me, bravely, I thought, with a ute, it was to the
Cape and the dark places of the Otway ridge that I returned to study the
night animals of the forest. Listening for the calls of masked owls, fishing
for crayfish by day, then returning to my little block and caravan for a feed,
before resuming my nocturnal habit.

Rohan Bilney

My PhD took me further from the place, to the Blue Mountains, where I studied predators, and even managed to include owls, this time replacing the screams of maskies with the falling-bomb whistle of the sooty owl.

By chance, the first job I got, after completing my PhD, contracting giardia and meeting my future wife at the Taj Mahal, was in Apollo Bay, at the foot of the Otway Range. And the second job I got was based on Cape Otway, and she was a desperately sad bit of country by then.

The Cape's true name, Bangerak, means 'knee of sand', or sand dunes. And it's a good name for a piece of country that is quite literally a series of stabilised wind-formed sand dunes. The eloquence and literality of that name will surprise no-one who understands the relationship between Aboriginal people and their country.

So for me, a trained wildlife biologist, it's not animals that make me human, it's country that does that. Because country is everything, including the totems and the people who live on her.

For me, a story of an encounter in the Colac area told by my friend and Kirrae Whurrong loreman John Clarke best describes how Indigenous Australians relate to their country. Settlers encounter a Gulidjan man who repeatedly points to himself and says 'Kolac gnat' to the Europeans. They mistakenly assume he is giving them the name of his tribe. But he is telling them this place, Kolac Kolac meaning 'much sand', is mine (I like to think he also muttered 'Piss off' under his breath but I'm sure he was far too polite). While in English these words are possessive, this was not how it was intended. He was saying this country is mine, in the same way he would say this is my friend, this is my family, this country is my kin.

We don't know a lot about the Gadabanud; in fact, the name itself is likely a derogatory term for the 'wild blacks' of the Otway ridge and the coastal fringe, given to them by the tribes of Maar to the west. It literally means 'speaking the king parrot tongue'. But from the lore holders of those Maar tribes, we know this term probably came about due to the very different languages of these tribal groups. We also know the Gadabanud likely intermarried and certainly traded with their neighbouring tribes. So the relationship was not hostile. We know they had established settlements on the Cape, and extensive middens along the coast that give us insight into part of their lifestyle. From historical records we also have a glimpse into how the Cape Otway woodlands looked under the tribe's care, and this resonated with the forests of my childhood, despite the area's history of grazing and hay cutting. It was when we stopped managing the woodlands entirely that they changed beyond recognition. People must be on country.

The first fire we lit was to encourage the gums to germinate. I was too in awe of the process of organising yellow overalls and red trucks to really pay attention. But the third fire we lit was huge, it didn't get away, we didn't destroy anything, but I knew it was not the right way. And in just the same way, now that we know more about fire on these dunes, when the smoke from our fires is light, I can feel the country breathe. I'm no master of fire lore, I still take plenty of missteps and I still occasionally light deliberately hot fires. But I can feel a growing lightness to the country as she sheds her coat of dense scrub and again reveals those gentle dunes. Those knees of sand.

So for me, a trained wildlife biologist, it's not animals that make me human, it's country that does that. Because country is everything, including the totems and the people who live on her. And it doesn't make me human so much as it shapes my life and sets out my responsibilities. It gives me my lore. And while Bangerak is not my traditional country, I know I have the responsibility to care for it, as it has played so great a role in my creation. And it's not really about me anyway, it's about the mother, because she doesn't recognise herself without her people. People acting within the bounds of their lore as dictated by story and custom. Story and custom that have been shaping the land management of this country for tens of thousands of years. I believe this is the only way we can heal damaged country and protect the mother.

Jack Pascoe grew up at Cape Otway, studied environmental science at Deakin University and completed a PhD with Western Sydney University, where he studied the predators of the Blue Mountains. Jack's key fields of interest are the ecology of apex predators and fire. Jack has worked in landcare and is currently chairperson of the Southern Otway Landcare Network. Jack is a Yuin man and is passionate about restoring cultural landscapes.

John
Woinarski

On becoming a pardalote

I've spent more of my life with pardalotes than with most other acquaintances. They are an obscure and odd group of four species of small (thumb-sized) birds. They have little public profile, not helped by the awkward name. But they are quintessentially Australian, occurring nowhere else in the world.

As a boy, I chanced upon a pair of spotted pardalotes absorbed in constructing their nesting burrow, a long tunnel built into sloping earth. Whereas most of the bird's existence is spent unobtrusively foraging in tree canopies, breeding brings this species to ground, allowing close observation by the quiet but inquisitive. My interest was piqued by their industry, beauty and strangeness. The intrigue stayed with me. Later, a PhD in zoology gave me the opportunity to study them in detail.

Zoology is a charmed science. Done well, it offers the opportunity to escape the conformity, constraints and solipsism of the human perspective; to see and understand the world from the viewpoint of another species, where space and time differ from the conventions we're used to, where the ordering of the importance of things is upended, where the elements of the natural world come far more sharply into focus and are imbued with different meanings. Zoology offers shapeshifting, and the insights that brings. It has taken me to many places, and a little into the diverse minds of remarkable species.

So, for three years I counted pardalotes at many sites and over many seasons.

Michael Livingston

Michael Livingston

I caught thousands, with wire-mesh traps at the entrances to their nesting burrows or with carefully sited nets. I attached leg bands, so I knew the identity of individuals. I weighed them, measured them, described the subtle variations in their jewelled plumage. I watched them for hours every day, recording the plant species in which they foraged, and what they ate. I studied their mating habits, their breeding success, their territoriality and social interactions. I reassessed my initial conception of them as placid when my experiments with a dummy pardalote and call playback triggered violent responses from territorial males. I examined the factors that threatened and killed them.

I found that they have long adapted to and exemplify an Australian ecology: they fit this country well. They forage almost entirely in eucalypts, that linchpin and defining feature of many Australian environments. Their diet is unusual, comprising mostly the sweet exudate (manna) that seeps from eucalypt foliage, and 'lerp', the sugary coating of psyllid insects

Michael Livingston

that suck the phloem from within that foliage. This strange resource is itself a consequence of the Australian environment – our soils are typically so poor that trees capturing nutrients must also drink up an excess of carbohydrates that they then need to secrete. The eucalypt– lerp–pardalote web is an intricate arrangement, played out in kaleidoscopic variation in different regions, with varying eucalypt, psyllid and pardalote species.

In the soundscape of my days, their intermittent call can still lure me away into lives that are not my own, into different ways of knowing our country and its workings.

Season adds a further dynamic to the landscape, with psyllid abundance diminishing in cooler areas in winter. So, like many other animal species, the pardalotes must track the ebb and flow of resources across our country, else stay put and starve. Indeed, episodes of mass mortality of pardalotes have been recorded in some winters. Some populations of these tiny birds cross formidable Bass Strait each year, heading from Tasmanian summers to the mainland for winter. Others disperse in a less orderly manner, nomadically tracking more unpredictable booms and busts of psyllid populations. Such nomadic movement is a distinctive feature of many Australian birds, contrasting markedly with the more rigid migration routes typical of birds on other continents – our seasonal patterning is more subtle and complex. But the ageless dispersal pathways of pardalotes have been subverted. Clearing has broken the continuity of the forests, rendering dispersal more hazardous. In little more than 200 years, about 40 per cent of their forest home has been destroyed, directly causing a comparable proportional loss in their population size.

Pardalotes have other threats. Around 10 per cent of their habitat was burned in the severe wildfires of 2019–20, with those fires most likely killing the birds directly, and leaving burned habitat unsuitable for their re-establishment for at least several years. In many parts of their range, the manner in which we have degraded and fragmented their forest and woodland habitat has benefitted a small suite of aggressive honeyeaters – the native noisy miner and bell miner – and these miners can kill pardalotes and exclude them from otherwise suitable habitat. Ecology is a complex network with many interwoven threads, and manipulation of one thread can have many reverberating impacts. We play with those threads at our peril.

From a human perspective, our land is mostly familiar, comforting.

But studying any Australian animal almost always leads to a crystallisation, a decipherment, of the destabilising manner in which we've contorted the ecology of this place. Purposefully, incompetently or haphazardly, we have rearranged the ecology of this land to suit our needs, and in doing so have rubbed away much that was integral to the existence of many other species. We are corroding our nature and will pass on to our descendants a land that is less healthy, less diverse, less wonderful.

Notwithstanding the less secure life most pardalotes now face, three pardalote species remain reasonably abundant and widespread. However, one species – the forty-spotted pardalote (a charming and apt name) – has been particularly hard-hit by the changes we have wrought to its environment. Now recognised as endangered, it has declined extensively and been reduced to a few populations (in beautiful locations) on some islands off Tasmania, with a fragile toehold at several small sites on the Tasmanian mainland. We still have the chance to save it, but that opportunity may soon be lost.

I no longer study pardalotes. But in the soundscape of my days, their intermittent call can still lure me away into lives that are not my own, into different ways of knowing our country and its workings, of the damage we've done and the healing we have yet to do.

John Woinarski is a professor of conservation biology at Charles Darwin University. He has been immersed in and fascinated with the wonder and beauty of Australia's nature since childhood. His research engages with the endless puzzle of the lives of other species. Much of this quest is focused on the ecology and conservation of threatened species and on trying to salve the environmental wounds we have inflicted on this country.

166

Michael Livingston

Leah Kaminsky

Wingy and Stormy

Oh, be kind to our web-footed friends
for a duck may be somebody's mother
A duck is at home in a swamp
which is always wet and damp
You may think it's the end of my song
Well, it is

——popular children's song

Hidden away for years, somewhere in the bowels of the offices of ASIO – the Australian Security Intelligence Organisation – was a secret dossier with my name stamped across the top. After the Freedom of Information Act was passed in Australia, I decided, out of sheer curiosity, to see if I was enough of a national threat to have come under the spy agency's radar. To my surprise, I received an official letter containing ASIO documents on which my name appeared. Not that I was any more radical than my fellow students in those days. Quite the opposite – I was usually the nerdy one. I had never been a member of any gang, I was too scared to attend protest rallies and, although I was too embarrassed to admit it to the cool kids at the time, I had never even smoked a joint. Turns out, the reason I was on the spy agency's watchlist was because of a duck.

The bird in question didn't have a name, nor had I ever met it. It was a

Gillian Rayment

native Pacific black duck (*Anas superciliosa*); a misnomer, because this Australian species actually has mostly brown plumage, with a shiny, bright-green patch tucked away under its wings. The black refers to the bold stripes that run from its bill to behind its eyes, making it look like it's headed to a fancy-dress party wearing a Zorro mask. Even though my particular duck was wild, I was sure it wasn't dangerous. In fact, it became my duck in the first place because it was being threatened by hunters. This happened at that time of year I came to hate in my home state of Victoria, the start of the official duck-hunting season, when 100,000 duck shooters would spend a fortune on camo gear and, in those days, semiautomatic rifles. They would wade out into pristine wetlands and shoot native waterfowl, often decimating an entire local population in one day, all in the name of sport. This infuriated me as a young student.

171

Gillian Rayment

Gillian Rayment

The real heroes in this story were a newly formed team of rescuers – the Coalition Against Duck Shooting – led by a quirky and courageous young agitator, Laurie Levy. They would rise at dawn and head off unarmed into the wetlands to ambush the shooters, trying to scare away the precious waterfowl with whistles and flags before too many rare, protected species became target practice for the day. I dreamt of joining the rescuers, but for someone with such a passion for protecting ducks, I was a chicken at heart. Instead, I decided to use some of the hard-earned cash I had set aside from waitressing at Sacco's Continental Delicatessen to sponsor a wild duck. My $4 an hour from working on Saturdays didn't amount to much of a contribution, but I wanted to feel like I was doing my bit to protect our native birds. Sadly, I had to rescind my sponsorship after several months, when the owner of the café fired me for accidentally spilling a bowl of hot soup onto a customer's lap. As soon as I started my new job as a medical intern, I renewed my duck sponsorship.

Ducks have always been a strong presence in my life, waddling through many stories and dreams, dabbling bottoms up for tidbits under the surface. I'm not sure when my love of ducks started, but it was more likely a result of watching cartoons after school than of any real encounters with animals in the wild. I wasn't an outdoorsy child. A flock of celebrity ducks populated my young imagination – Disney's temperamental Donald Duck and his girlfriend, Daisy, together with their naughty nephews Huey, Dewey and Louie; Looney Tunes' sassy Daffy Duck; and Beatrix Potter's headstrong Jemima Puddle-Duck, always looking for a safe place to lay her eggs. I identified strongly with 'The Ugly Duckling', looking in the mirror at my prominent bat ears and wondering if one day I might emerge as a beautiful, fearless woman/swan.

I collected duck tchotchkes and toys. My favourite, Shloimie Bellini, a white porcelain duck, still sits on my shelf, smiling knowingly, his surname borrowed from the artist's sticker on his hollow belly. He was a twenty-first birthday present from my mother, who died two months later. I like to think Shloimie

I am content to sit peacefully on the banks of the local lake, watching bossy old Stormy chase Wingy away by nipping at her tail feathers, or marvelling at how quickly the Thirteen Attributes have learnt to swim, while their watchful parents corral them protectively.

was a substitute for the pet duck she had never let me have. Nowadays, I am content to sit peacefully on the banks of the local lake, watching bossy old Stormy chase Wingy away by nipping at her tail feathers, or marvelling at how quickly the Thirteen Attributes have learnt to swim, while their watchful parents corral them protectively. I love it when they turn topsy-turvy, plunging their heads underwater, bottoms pointed to the sky, their little webbed feet flapping madly in the air. They are foraging for the seeds of aquatic plants, with the odd insect or mollusc thrown into the mix.

Instead of venturing out into the field with Laurie Levy's group to fight the shooters back in the eighties, I chose the safer option and signed up as an armchair activist. That one act of subversion turned me into an instant radical in ASIO's opinion, seemingly a potential threat to the very fabric of Australian society. I think they had their eyes on the wrong person. With a 90 per cent reduction in waterbird numbers since the eighties, Victoria is the only state left in Australia in which duck shooters can still legally hunt. I will continue to raise my voice to help protect our web-footed friends. You may think it's the end of my song. Well, it isn't.

Leah Kaminsky is a physician and award-winning writer. Her debut novel, *The Waiting Room*, won the Voss Literary Prize. *The Hollow Bones* won both the Literary Fiction and Historical Fiction categories of the 2019 International Book Awards, and the 2019 American Book Fest's Best Book Award for Literary Fiction. She is the author of ten books and holds an MFA from Vermont College of Fine Arts.

Mark Brandi

The dusk flight

Throughout childhood, I had a fraught relationship with my ethnicity, occupying a nether world between Italian and Australian, but never feeling I belonged to either. This unease played out in the schoolyard, where sporting allegiances were a de facto test of patriotism. So while I pretended to enjoy our nation's success on the sporting field, the reality was very different.

From the safety of my family's lounge room, I quietly barracked for the West Indies cricket team, cheered Ivan Lendl's cool dispassion against Pat Cash, and cringed at the jingoism around our America's Cup success. To my young eyes, kangaroos' and koalas' roles as sporting mascots made them guilty by association.

In country Victoria, where I grew up, these animals were a subtle part of the landscape, rarely seen. But with the Grampians National Park close by, they were used by some as a tourist drawcard, and one motel even went with a supersized Giant Koala – a terrifying fibreglass beast, looming large over the Western Highway.

But my first sighting of actual wildlife was in the astonished presence of my maternal grandparents, visiting our country for the very first time. While driving through the Grampians, my dad spotted two koalas lounging in a gum tree. Keen to impress his father-in-law, he pulled the Kingswood over to the side of the road.

'Incredible, aren't they?' he said, smiling with pride.

Vivien Jones

Vivien Jones

I smiled too. But in truth, I found it difficult to feel proud of anything associated with Australianness, let alone our wildlife.

Indeed, much of my contact with animals was limited to yabbying and fishing, or took place through the scope of a rifle. Looking back, there was a distinctly violent flavour to my interaction with the natural world. Life in rural Australia seemed akin to Kenneth Cook's *Wake in Fright* – a desolate, testosterone-fuelled world of blood and brutality. As soon as I was able, I moved to the city, and my connection with nature remained distant.

There is, however, one exception.

Oddly enough, it's an animal I was terrified of as a kid, mostly thanks to the horror films I shouldn't have been watching. But these creatures are less sinister than the Hammer Film variety, even if lovers of fig trees might disagree.

In Melbourne's inner city, a large colony of fruit bats nests in Yarra Bend Park. At dusk they can be seen in their thousands, flying across the suburbs in the falling light. Many land in the backyards of my neighbours, munching through what once were the gardens of migrants such as my parents, now gentrified and sculpted.

And even though I've always loved homegrown fruit, the bats' mass flight leaves me in awe of our natural world, and our small place within it.

One evening just recently, while walking my dog, I came across a young French tourist standing on the footpath, her camera pointed towards the sky.

We both stood together for a moment, each of us once from the other side of the planet, watching in quiet wonder as these creatures passed through the clouded twilight.

'Incredible, aren't they?' she said, smiling brightly.

'Yes,' I agreed. 'They really are.'

Mark Brandi's bestselling novel, *Wimmera* (Hachette Australia), won the Crime Writers' Association's Debut Dagger (UK) and the Indie Book Award for Debut Fiction, and has been shortlisted for numerous prizes. His second novel, *The Rip*, has been longlisted for the Best Fiction category of the Crime Writers' Association's 2019 Ned Kelly Awards and for Best Fiction Novel at the 2020 Indie Book Awards.

Shaun
Tan

Pippi Eugene

When a red wattlebird mistakes my ear for a flower, inserting its scimitar beak and darting tongue down the canal, the sound is deafening. A staccato drumbeat, a tiny nectar-seeking bullet. Soon realising how little sustenance my ear affords, this wiry bird settles for a quick drink from the corner of my mouth. Am I like the sappy split in the fork of a tree? A rivulet of moisture in the crack of a rock? Or the faint echo of its mother's mouth, feeding it in the nest it fell from?

I was about eleven years old, taking a shortcut through a dark neck of the local park, on my way to a friend's birthday party, glittery card and hastily wrapped box of Lego in hand. A scrum of squawks and feathers passed overhead, one of numerous bird wars that seemed so elemental to the canopies of Perth's northern suburbs, peppered as they were in those days with twisting, shaggy masses of tuart trees, alive with raucous life. Back then those trees were so ugly to me, so irregular and graceless. Unclimbable. Rough as guts. Prone to spiders and other insects for which phobias are just waiting to be invented. The cursed home of broody magpies, the great dread of spring, and all those other volatile birds.

But much later, when I started painting my local landscape as an art student (too lazy to seek out more exotic subjects), I came to know these trees quite differently. I studied their bent masses of foliage, rising and hanging, forming caves or mouths, arcades and towers marking specific districts, thoroughfares,

Michael Livingston

places to meet, hide, nest, negotiate, all shifting with the rake of a golden westerly in the afternoon. Taking time to look – the true purpose of drawing and painting – I saw another neighbourhood above my own, another country, a vast empire of birds. In comparison to the structurally flimsy pretensions of human suburbia – a flat sprawl that survived only by the good grace of plumbing, petrol and electrical wires strung everywhere like confessions of a conceptual weakness impossible to hide – these tree worlds were *old*. They were all that remained of the original coastal plain, but boy did they remain. When painting tuarts from the roof of my parents' house, I came to realise how old all of the land really was. And also, how interrupted it was by humans.

As a child, though, I probably more often felt the opposite. That humans were interrupted by nature. All this scrubby bush, well, if a bulldozer happened to come along (which they did seem to do, every other week), then good riddance. Too many bugs, too much sand, too many wasps, flies and bees; gum leaves so stiff and flat on a driveway that no broom could move them; and an army of ants just waiting to rise up and overthrow us. Postcolonial hubris runs very deep and is so quietly transgenerational that you can't even see it, being too busy sweeping and whingeing, retreating indoors to read books about English gardens and Germanic fairytale forests. Too busy trying to get to a birthday party, worried about missing a piñata or some other fun cultural confusion.

But when a small wattlebird fell from a tuart tree in front of me, literally in front my gaffer-taped Kmart sneakers, some deeper empathy snapped to attention, a compassion that bypassed all other thinking, a sense of kinship and purpose. The ruckus of birds ripping into each other moved on to another canopy, and I dutifully waited near this crashed aviator to see what would happen. It floundered about, a fluffy, dull-coloured heap on the quiet grass. Clearly just a fledgling, perhaps it had strayed into the wrong territory, or escaped a crow. I knew enough to diagnose a broken wing. It would never get back to the nest, this little snack for local cats and dogs. I bundled the bird carefully in my T-ball cap, mindful that you weren't supposed to touch a bird with your hands (I couldn't remember why), and ran all the way home, quietly pleased. The dark and ugly tuart trees had chosen me to save this bird. The birthday party could wait.

Our family was not unfamiliar with stray and injured animals, even had a penchant for collecting them. A deformed goldfish, a myopic cat, and a budgie with a severe underbite that my mum bought from a pet shop only because she was sure nobody else would. There was another stray cat, Marmalade, who wandered blithely in and out of classrooms at my primary school until our principal, a man possibly more at home hunting feral animals in the bush, openly threatened to knock it over the head with a shovel and dispose of the body in a hessian sack – over the PA system, no less. On the matter of injury, it did not help that my architect father had designed our home with groovy high windows that proved a deathtrap for local birds. You would hear three inevitable sounds: first, the bird braining itself on an impossibly solid piece of sky; second, the body falling onto the galvanised roof below; third, a cat (the one with full vision) running as fast as it could to reach the fallen bird before we intervened with a ladder. It was always a race to get there first. Half the time, the stunned birds just needed protection, needed the cat to be warded off with a broom until they could recover and fly away, or be removed from the hot roof and placed into a shoebox for a while. The rest of the time, the acute angle of the neck signalled it was time to add another tiny gravestone to our animal cemetery under the mango tree, where turtles, fish, canaries, budgies, crayfish and sundry other species lay, a nice little puzzle for some future palaeontologist.

As a child, though, I probably more often felt the opposite. That humans were interrupted by nature. All this scrubby bush, well, if a bulldozer happened to come along (which they did seem to do, every other week), then good riddance.

184

So, it was no surprise to be bringing home an injured bird, although we'd never seen a wattlebird so close before; they seemed to us such wild and uncatchable creatures. We didn't really know what to do with this species, so my mum rang Perth Zoo. They were very helpful and explained how to feed it a combination of some milky mush and strips of raw beef rolled in crushed dog kibble, which seemed strange as we'd only ever witnessed these birds sucking on the bottlebrush flowers in our driveway. Either way, the zoo did not fancy our poor bird's chances, and neither did we.

But those zoo people knew their stuff, and it worked. Naturally timid at first, the small bird soon guzzled our weird offerings, taking the eye-dropper and tweezers so far down its tiny throat – like its mother's beak,

Shaun Tan

we supposed – you wondered how it didn't choke. It jackhammered food directly into its crop, the capacity of which you could see just by looking at the fluffy bulge. It stayed in its shoebox, never looking entirely well, but not quite dying either. Its beady black eyes were, at least, always bright. Its wing was still a bit misaligned, but would flap and fold as it strengthened, and even wiggle with anticipation when it wanted more food.

Many injured birds had died in our shoeboxes over the years, so we were quite surprised to witness the recovery of this one, how it moved willingly onto a perch and watched us knowingly with quick, sharp movements. We were careful not to spend too much time with it, wanting to return it to the tuarts as soon as possible, with minimal

How the tiny red ear-wattles had the vermilion-coloured wrinkles of a red-cap gum pod just before the flower burst out. The faint dusting of yellow pollen between its eucalyptus- twig legs.

human taint. Counting on this prompt repatriation, I gave the bird a silly onomatopoeic name that wouldn't matter. *Pippi* was its pipette-like head, the surgical precision of its movements, and *Eugene* was the soft guttural sound of its juvenile squawk. I've yet to name another animal as absurdly and perfectly as this one, Pippi Eugene, knowing that our time together would not last. For one thing, as the zoo staff had informed us, it was illegal to keep a wild native animal as a pet.

Accordingly, as soon as Pippi Eugene was strong enough, we moved him to an outdoor tree, continuing to feed him by hand. Introducing him to flowers of a kind we had seen other wattlebirds eat, we showed him where to find them independently. We discovered that he also enjoyed the occasional drop of honey in a bottle cap, and that caterpillars were his favourite, especially if they were still in a cocoon. Pippi Eugene sometimes 'asked' us to cut the ends off with scissors to allow easy access, after we had demonstrated to him that we giant apes could do such a thing much more effectively than a stabbing beak.

Pippi began to disappear during the day, fending for himself and doing whatever it is that wattlebirds do. But often he would fly down from the canopies of trees to sit on our heads, hands or shoulders for a while, sticking his beak in our ear or mouth. It was never clear if this was a gesture of affection. It may have been that the bird was simply hardwired to check anything remotely floral for water and calories, things of some scarcity in the semi-arid forests of its ancestry. Up close, you could feel the complex unity of an animal with its environment, a physical poetry. The way its clean feathers smelt faintly of sea breeze and herring, just like the wild, windy beaches down the road. How the tiny red ear-wattles had the vermilion-coloured wrinkles of a red-cap gum pod just before the flower burst out. The faint dusting of yellow pollen between its eucalyptus-twig legs. The plumage that looked like a piece of bark slightly scorched at the top by bushfire, the eyes like hardened resin. This was an animal, a very old animal, a very old piece of land. Like all such creatures, Pippi sensed everything around him acutely, things we domesticated blow-ins would never notice. His eyesight, his ability to notice minuscule detail, was particularly remarkable. If you found a cocoon, you only had to hold it in your open palm and Pippi Eugene would fly down from some distant tree, a small approaching dot, enlarging just long enough to land on your hand, gobble up the poor aspiring butterfly, and skip away.

At the end of each day, Pippi Eugene returned to the same spot in our courtyard tree, painting a nice Jackson Pollock, *Red Wattlebird No. 2*, on the pavement below. It became our evening ritual to check that Pippi was there every night before we turned in to bed. It felt like the perfect human–animal relationship. We did not own Pippi, and Pippi was not at all dependent upon us, he could come and go as he pleased. He was a wild bird that we just happened to know. We had succeeded in our duty.

Then one day the cat got him. The cat that had escaped the shovel and hessian sack of our school principal and, truth be told, was a ruthless killer and perhaps should never have been brought home by us well-intentioned kids. The cat who, for so many years, had been denied the fruits of those groovy high windows. Who had been watching Pippi for months from behind glass and flyscreen, far beneath the bird's sleeping perch, artfully pretending that he couldn't care less. And Pippi, for his part, was always too comfortable around big mammals, and perhaps this was the one weakness of his rehabilitation. I saw the whole thing unfold at the end of our driveway: an orange blur, a shaking shrub, a soft squawk – *Eugene!* – and there was Marmalade, a fan of long tail feathers protruding from his mouth, looking as surprised as anyone else at

I saw the whole thing unfold at the end of our driveway: an orange blur, a shaking shrub, a soft squawk – Eugene!

188

this unlikely stroke of luck. I felt immediate guilt. I, the chosen protector, had failed. Or else had simply delayed a death already scripted by fate.

How relieved I was then to see the very same bird, Pippi Eugene, later sitting on the edge of the garage roof, bold as brass, with nothing on his backside but a downy tuft. Another survivalist trick of the wily wattlebird: knowing when to drop your arse and run. The tail grew back over the coming weeks, and Pippi steered clear of cats from then on. I suppose his education was now complete.

We did not see him very much after that. He no longer slept by the window. He still visited our heads and shoulders, but less and less, and then we didn't see him at all. The seasons passed and the complex territorial wars of suburban birds carried on. Crows, magpies, willie wagtails, honeyeaters, twenty-eight parrots, galahs, the odd kookaburra, and those wattlebirds, all identical to Pippi Eugene with their red ear-wattles and pale flush of yellow, but never quite sounding the same. Always more brusque and aloof, always regarding our offering of a cocoon with a blank gaze. When you looked past the beautiful bird calls, it was a harsh and politically violent universe, and our family accepted that Pippi may well be dead out there. We would simply never know, and fair enough too. He was never our pet; he was never ours at all.

When the paths of strangers cross, we have an opportunity to see something of ourselves more clearly. Especially our more compassionate selves, the ones that know, without much wisdom or forethought, that you are supposed to rescue an injured bird and do as much as possible to get it back to an ugly old tree.

The story of Pippi would have ended there, if not for a fortuitous little postscript. About a year later, my parents noticed a wattlebird sitting in our front yard, unusually bold, and naturally wondered if it might be the one and only Pippi Eugene. They brought out a bottle top with a little honey in it. The bird recognised this immediately and hopped close to lap it up with that staccato tongue. Yes, it was Pippi, and better still, he appeared to have a mate. As my folks tell it, it was as if he was visiting one last time to show us that things had turned out fine, to proudly introduce a spouse.

It's certainly heartening to think so. Then again, maybe some faint territorial recollection drew him back, a distant memory of sweetness, or more likely, nothing we can ever properly imagine at all. Does it matter what animals think, and what we think they think? I've pondered this for years, writing and painting and walking around suburbia with a camera and sketchbook, paying special attention to birds, trying to imagine the paths and meanings they follow between wires and trees. Wondering about the strange ways that affection can exist across an evolutionary divide, between creatures whose landscapes are so separate but so intertwined, somehow bound to a single plane of existence by the accidents of history. We can't know each other fully and it might be foolish to think we can even know each other at all. But when the paths of strangers cross, we have an opportunity to see something of ourselves more clearly. Especially our more compassionate selves, the ones that know, without much wisdom or forethought, that you are supposed to rescue an injured bird and do as much as possible to get it back to an ugly old tree.

Shaun Tan grew up in Perth and works as an artist, writer and filmmaker in Melbourne. He is best known for illustrated books that deal with social and historical subjects through dream-like imagery. *The Rabbits*, *The Red Tree*, *Tales from Outer Suburbia*, *Rules of Summer* and the graphic novel *The Arrival* have been widely translated throughout the world and enjoyed by readers of all ages. Shaun is the recipient of an Academy Award for the short animated film *The Lost Thing* and the prestigious Astrid Lindgren Memorial Award in Sweden.

190

Claire G. Coleman

That wirlo cry

The September sun was setting on the day of the official launch of my debut novel, *Terra Nullius*. I was beyond exhausted – I had spoken at the Brisbane Writers Festival sometime during the day and had only managed to find a couple of hours in the green room to rest. Then I had launched my book, an hour-long event in the heat of a temporary structure, when already weary.

Brisbane was quiet, slipping away into the warmish glow of evening. I had agreed to another event, a talk around a fire pit, only half an hour after my launch, when I would rather have been eating dinner, drinking bubbles, anything other than talking more.

In Brisbane it feels like the twilight lingers, holding on in the warm subtropical air, more than it does in my ancestral Noongar country or in Naarm, where I spend most of my days. I sat down at the end of the space, took the microphone in hand and prepared to talk, then fell silent. The air had been filled with a cacophony of blood-chilling screams, a wall of noise that might have come from hell itself.

It was the distinct, unmistakable cry of the bush stone-curlew, called wirlo in Noongar, the language of my Aboriginal ancestors from the south coast of Western Australia. Actually it was a chorus of screams from more wirlo than I have ever heard in one chorus, before or after, more than I have ever seen in one place; perhaps more than I will ever see in one place.

Georgina Steytler

Georgina Steytler

The wirlo is a complicated bird, culturally. To many Aboriginal people I know, it is the 'devil bird' who steals men, leading them away to their death, who steals children from the safety of their parents' arms; or the 'death bird', a harbinger of death whose cry is a warning. Those are the oral histories of that beautiful bird, whose song is like no other bird's on earth; so like human screaming yet so unearthly.

They do sound like a devil, or a screaming child, or a wailing mother.

To my family they have a very different meaning, however. Oral history, from the family who claim my family, identifies us as the Wirlomin, the people of the wirlo.

When first I saw a wirlo it was not in the wild. They are now rare in my ancestral country. Land clearing, logging, livestock and foxes, mostly foxes, have taken a huge toll on these ground-nesting, almost flightless birds. A nature park south of Townsville had some in cages, forlorn, camouflaged against the scraps of plants in their enclosure. One performed in their Free Flying Bird Show, running full tilt through the crowd, chasing the food thrown for him. Even at a free-flying show the wirlo refused to fly.

It was not in my country that I first saw wirlo in the wild either, it was in Townsville. We parked our caravan to go to the NAIDOC celebration and a wirlo family living in the gnarled roots of a Moreton Bay fig seemed intent on greeting us. After that they came into my life frequently.

On the night of my book launch in Brisbane it felt like the wirlo were cheering my success. Despite the fact that I was in public, being watched, my breath caught in my throat; my tears fell.

Just north of Townsville there's a rest area attached to a park, where it's legal to sleep in a motorhome or caravan for a night or so. There, living in that park, is a particularly cheeky wirlo – my partner and I call him (or her – I never learnt to tell wirlo sexes apart) Mr Yelly. Every time we visit that park we see him, he's one of the highlights of travelling through Queensland; he's why I want to return to Queensland right now.

They have a delightful way of running, wirlo, carrying themselves like miniature emus but somehow more gangly; like a shrunk-down

To me they are family, they are special but they are more than that. They are my favourite family; my favourite cousins. Even the thought of wirlo makes me happy, and that is special.

emu on stilts; a bit like the cartoon character Road Runner, if he had the attitude of the Tasmanian devil. I smile when I see wirlo, I am warmed when I see one run full tilt across a park, perhaps in hot pursuit of something edible. Mr Yelly lives in a park under lights, perhaps having learnt that the light calls the bugs. He stands there sometimes in the pool of the park lights, surrounded by darkness; sometimes, standing there, he screams.

He scares the shit out of backpackers when he screams at the top of his lungs with no warning.

One night I had stopped in the middle of the park, on the way to the toilet block, when I saw him running across the road. Stopping under the window of a darkly silent caravan, he let rip, screaming that piercing cry. I don't know what the people in the caravan thought was going on but there was a clatter and a thump and all the lights flashed on one by one.

But Mr Yelly was gone, storming off into the darkness, his natural environment, on his lanky legs, hunting frogs and bugs with those huge, beautiful, intelligent eyes and strong beak.

In Cairns, wirlo run and fight and yell all through the esplanade park, crossing the road on occasion to the café strip, looking for something special to eat. Many people, locals and tourists alike, fail to notice these beautiful birds until they are in the spaces humans occupy, until they are, in fact, running down the footpath, big-eyed, lanky and human-knee height.

Most Australians don't know wirlo exist; they are large birds, but being mostly nocturnal and mostly ground-dwelling in the bush, they are not easy to find. When confronted by humans or predators they freeze, looking like a stick, an impression they are famously good at; or if they are in genuine danger they outstretch their wings and charge.

To me they are family, they are special but they are more than that. They are my favourite family; my favourite cousins. Even the thought of wirlo makes me happy, and that is special.

Claire G. Coleman is a Wirlomin Noongar novelist, playwright and poet whose family has belonged to the south coast of Western Australia since long before history started being recorded. Her first novel, *Terra Nullius*, won a black&write! Indigenous Writing Fellowship and was shortlisted for the Stella Prize. Her latest novel is *The Old Lie*.

Georgina Steytler

Favel Parrett

Asking for welcome

My steps become even, easy
In rhythm
A heartbeat
And time slows down

A magpie song
A currawong call
A welcome

A few years ago, I started bushwalking by myself, because the call of the wild had become so overwhelming that I just couldn't wait for other people. I had to go on my own.

At first, I was a bit nervous. Not about snakes or getting lost, but about other people. There is nothing more frightening than coming across some lone human who has set up an end-of-days camp in the middle of nowhere. It's like a classic Australian horror story, one that haunts your dreams. But the urgency of needing to be in the bush was strong enough for me to step through my fears. One thing helped greatly – asking for welcome. Asking for welcome has become a steadfast ritual before I set foot on any trail. I ask the Elders, the First Australians, the *true* custodians of this land, for welcome. I say over and over, 'I come in peace and with an open heart – I ask for

Peter Taylor

welcome on your land.' Then I wait for a sign. Sometimes it is just the wind, the creak of a tree, a soft bird call. My favourite sign is the song of a pied currawong. That always feels like a blessing to me. The pied currawong has become my good-luck charm and I feel happy whenever I hear one.

I tried shorter walks, ones that I knew well. I was building my confidence, my solo navigation skills. But once my nerves settled and I got into the rhythm of walking, everything changed. Everything calmed down. I just listened. I was just in the moment and time slowed.

When you are walking with other people, it's easy to miss so much. Talking takes you away somewhere else – to the past, the future, the concrete world of the human being. Talking also scares off wildlife. But when I am walking solo, if I listen carefully enough, I feel like I can even hear the trees speaking to me. And I do listen. I do listen to trees. They have a lot to tell us.

I see so much more when I walk alone. I have had some of the closest and most special encounters with wildlife on my solo walks. From echidnas to wedge-tailed eagles to swamp wallabies, to bandicoots – no encounter is too small to fill my heart with joy. Seeking out these moments has become vital to me. More and more, the wild is the only thing that truly matters, and when I am away from it for too long I grow listless. I can't write, I can't dream. I just don't feel like me.

Recently, I was lucky enough to receive a writing residency on the edge of Sherbrooke Forest, called the Jacky Winter Residency. It was heaven. I spent as much time as I could walking in the national park and thinking, as well as writing. I completely fell in love with the majestic forest of mountain ash – tall and ancient and like some kind of fairytale. So different to the ironbark forests I know so well on the Surf Coast where I live. I could have stayed for months and been completely happy in that forest.

On my last full day at the residency, I set out before sunrise in the hope of seeing as much wildlife as I could. I especially hoped I would see a lyrebird – a bird I had never seen in the wild before. And I really did get lucky. I saw five lyrebirds that morning, four males and one female. The last encounter lasted for over thirty minutes, as I sat down on a log and watched a

More and more, the wild is the only thing that truly matters, and when I am away from it for too long I grow listless. I can't write, I can't dream. I just don't feel like me.

dashing male prance back and forth right next to me. He scratched with his large, sharp talons, moving sticks and rocks and the dark earth to get at his breakfast. He was not afraid of me, his old dinosaur eyes finding mine from time to time. His dainty and beautiful full-feathered tail even brushed the skin on my arm a few times. It is an experience I will never forget.

Right now, our natural environment is in crisis and it is screaming at us. It is screaming so loudly that the sound is deafening. But we try so hard to drown it out, to pretend that everything is fine. We distract ourselves – we shop till we drop – we fill our days with bright shiny screens and we refuse to listen.

This is exactly why connecting with the wild is more important than it has ever been.

Being in the wild is where we can listen.
Being in the wild is where we can be human.

I sit down and this place hums through me
I rest my hand against the earth
There are clear marks of an echidna's digging, digging – sniffing
A midnight feast
A beam of sunlight shoots through the canopy
And two rosellas rush past me – talking, talking
They fly up, up towards the light
I breathe in deeply
I breathe out
I close my eyes
I can feel it all

200

Favel Parrett's career was launched with her critically acclaimed debut, *Past the Shallows*, which was shortlisted for the prestigious Miles Franklin Literary Award and won the Dobbie Literary Award. Favel herself won the ABIA Newcomer of the Year Award in 2012. Her next novel, *When the Night Comes*, was also critically acclaimed and further consolidated Favel's reputation with booksellers and readers. Her most recent novel, *There Was Still Love*, was shortlisted for the 2020 Stella Prize. Favel's short stories have been published in various journals and magazines including *Island*, *Griffith Review* and *Frankie*.

James Bradley

A visitor

I n 2003 my partner and I moved to an apartment in Bondi. Because the beach was only a couple of hundred metres away – so close, in fact, that when storms washed through you could see the spray drifting over the building – the trees out the front were what you would expect – scrubby grevilleas, a couple of palms, the melaleucas that lined the kerb. But out the back, hidden from the street, the garden we shared with our neighbours might as well have been a different world, its lawn surrounded by massive gums and crepe myrtles, in the shade of which grew lilies and other flowering plants.

I worked in the sunroom at the front, looking out over the street through a big bottlebrush. During the day a parade of birds fed on its flowers: lorikeets that clowned and clamoured as they clambered drunkenly about in the leaves, noisy miners eager for confrontation, wary wattlebirds, apt to dart away if disturbed.

Out the back there were even more birds: not just smaller birds like honeyeaters and pardalotes, but also figbirds and glossy black drongos, and in the summers, koels and other cuckoos. There were even owls from time to time: early one morning I was woken by the sound of something striking the back window; concerned, I ran down the hall to find the currawongs that lived in the garden sitting in the trees, watching me through the glass. For a second or two I stood in silence, aware something had happened, or perhaps

Craig Coverdale

was still happening, before, without warning, a barn owl rose up silently directly in front of me, its pale shape ghostly in the pre-dawn light, and disappeared over the building, pursued by the currawongs.

In the time we lived in that apartment I came to know those currawongs, which nested in the trees above our clothesline. Once their chicks fledged, they would call all day, creaking and rasping in the branches while their parents watched us for any sign of danger. But the birds I became most attached to were the magpies.

Although many people fear magpies for their habit of swooping during nesting season, I have always loved them. Growing up in Adelaide, their morning carolling was a constant, and even today it reminds me of my childhood and adolescence, evoking memories of my father's house in Glenelg, and the huge pine tree a few doors down in which the magpies would congregate.

During our first summer in our apartment in Bondi, a pair of magpies nested in the tree outside the building next door. Although I could not see their nest from my study, I could hear them calling, and when I walked to the shop on the corner, I would often see the parents patrolling the grass beneath it. Eventually the chicks appeared, descending clumsily into the lower boughs of the trees and eventually onto the ground, their movements carefully monitored by their watchful parents.

Telling magpies apart is difficult. Although they may live to be twenty or thirty years old, and will usually inhabit a particular territory for most of their adult life, meaning the magpie you see in your backyard every day is almost certainly the same magpie you've been seeing for years, even decades, individual birds tend to look very much the same. Yet one of the birds in this brood was immediately recognisable by the fact the plumage on her left side was almost entirely black, instead of the black and white (or black and white and speckled grey) it should have been.

Because she was so striking, I would often stop to talk to her when I saw her in the street. And in time she – and her parents – grew used to me, and although they never approached me, came to seem perfectly comfortable with my presence.

In a way this shouldn't have been surprising: magpies are highly intelligent, and not only can they recognise and remember individual humans, they often form friendships with them, visiting them for food and even allowing their human friends to touch them.

But then, one day, my magpie friend was gone, presumably chased away by her parents as is the way in magpie society. At first I was sorry not to see her every day, but after a while I stopped thinking about it, until one day, a few months later, she reappeared, this time in our garden and in the company of another, larger magpie I assumed must be her mate. I was delighted, especially since she seemed to have claimed the area as her own.

Over the next couple of years, I spent a lot of time with my asymmetrical friend: when I stood on our deck looking out at the trees or went downstairs to hang the clothes on the line, I would watch her and talk to her, enchanted by the obvious intelligence with which she regarded me in return.

Finally, in our fourth or fifth summer there, she built a nest, and laid eggs, and within a few weeks she and her mate had a brood of their own. Delighted, I watched the chicks get bigger and begin to fly. And then, one morning when I was working in our back room with the doors open to the deck, I heard a clacking on the boards. I looked around and was startled to see her standing in our kitchen, only a metre or so from where I sat, her now reasonably sizeable chicks in a line behind her. I fell still. She didn't seem agitated or confused. Instead she just stood there with her chicks, staring at me.

A few moments passed. I knew something significant was taking place, that some meaning was being communicated, if not to me, then to the chicks. Then, calmly and unhurriedly, she turned around and led the chicks back out the door and onto the deck, whatever she had come to do accomplished.

I don't know what she thought she was doing: perhaps it was just coincidence that she was there that day. But I suspect it was something else, something she was telling her chicks, something about me. I would like to think it was that I was a friend, a person to be trusted, but perhaps it was simply that I was harmless. Either way, some meaning seemed to have passed between us, a moment of recognition captured in the steady regard of her dark-orange eyes.

James Bradley is a novelist and critic. His books include the novels *Wrack*, *The Deep Field*, *The Resurrectionist*, *Clade* and *Ghost Species*. His work has won or been shortlisted for a number of major Australian and international literary awards and has been widely translated. He lives in Sydney.

Angela Meyer

Temporary visitors

I watched the bird of prey circling low over the grass and treetops of the undulating valleys behind my parents' house in Lowanna, northern New South Wales. This behaviour, I now know, is called 'quartering': systematically hunting area by area. Sometimes the bird would perch on a fence post or tree branch, preening while surveying the ground. I first noticed it in a tree, on one of my recent visits, a little while after the smoke had cleared from the bushfires that came close to the area. I couldn't identify it initially, my time and attention mainly occupied with my dad's illness, and work.

On my next visit, it flew right up to the house and I gasped at the spectacular rust-warm underbody, the smoke-tipped 'fingers' and the striped, fanned tail. It was the tail that helped me figure out what it was. A spotted harrier, of the family Accipitridae; its nickname 'smoke hawk'.

The spotted harrier is widely dispersed throughout Australia and Indonesia, particularly in arid or semi-arid areas. I wondered if this particular bird had chosen the area near my parents' house during the unprecedented long period without rain before and during the fire season. This is normally a lush valley, on the west bank of the Little Nymboida River, in the Coffs Coast hinterland. It is not uncommon to wake up to a heavy mist coating the land. I wondered if the hawk would stay put now that there had been downfalls and floods.

There certainly was plenty of food for it here – terrestrial birds, rodents, reptiles, large insects and, in the valley, an abundance of lizards and snakes,

Georgina Steytler

massive praying mantises and crickets.

I wondered if it was alone or had a mate. Could it be hunting for its family, or quartering those fields to satisfy its own appetite?

One day my dad saw it up close from the window by his bed and thought it had reddish streaks on its underparts. Apparently juveniles have brown streaks across the chest and stomach, so we felt it may be young. Adult birds progress from streaks to white spots.

I reached out to bird-of-prey expert Stephen Debus. He said from my photo it appeared to be an adult, 'or nearly so', as the juveniles are brown on top with extensive ginger shoulders and undersides.

He also said a spotted harrier occurring at Lowanna was 'exceptional', and he explained it was most likely a drought refugee from inland, or a migrant passing through.

He confirmed its hunting pattern: 'They do typically quarter fields for small prey in tall ground vegetation, using their owl-like facial ruff to pinpoint the sounds of prey rustling, and reaching it with their long legs.' He said that in southern Australia the hawks breed in spring and summer and head north for the winter. The bird we'd seen was likely a 'temporary visitor' that might remain while it could find food.

The spotted harrier is listed as 'vulnerable' in New South Wales, with at least a 30 per cent reduction in the population over three generations as a result of the clearing and degradation of its habitat, with the subsequent decrease in available prey.

In the five years my parents have lived here, the area has not changed a lot. It is accessed by a winding mountain road through partly subtropical rainforest. In recent rains, we were trapped here by landslides for several days. The population is small. Once, this area was more populous than coastal Coffs Harbour, when it was a centre for the timber industry. Blackbutt, tallowwood and hoop pine were extensively milled, and gold was also mined.

Birds are mentioned in a casual observation of a local, Clare Hampton, from 1956–57: 'Gouldian finches, rifle bird, scrub turkeys, black and sulphur-crested cockatoos, wood ducks, lyre bird, king parrots, rosellas, blue mountain parrots, wonga and wood pigeons, coachwhip, butcher birds, peewits, wagtails, wrens, honey eaters, quail, dab chicks, cranes, ibis, eagle and chicken hawks, magpies, kookaburras, dollar birds and plover'. I've seen around 70 per cent of these birds in recent months.

And it's not only the birds of prey who have enjoyed the taste of reptiles in the area. In 1942 a Special Army Training Centre with 600 trainees was set up in Lowanna by a Major G. A. Crawford. Mel Ward, a naturalist from Sydney University, joined the major's staff for several weeks. 'His profound knowledge of nature and all things appertaining to the bush, the birds and creatures that live therein, was imparted to the troops by way of lectures and demonstrations of how to live off the land; how to prepare and bake a carpet snake on a cone of mud was one of his most popular demonstrations and one in which the troops were keenly interested.'

Many place names around here are from the Gumbaynggyirr language (Lowanna meaning 'girl'). The word for a large bird in Gumbaynggyirr is jiibinygany, and I want to acknowledge the extended relationship the Indigenous owners have with the country on which I write this.

This country will always have meaning for me, because this is where my dad died. A few days before, I glanced at the smoke hawk through the window, but thought I saw two of them. It seemed a bit too amazing, so I dismissed it in my mind. But after Dad died, I saw, undeniably, that the spotted harrier had a mate. I saw him fly under her in the air, chattering, and it felt like I was witnessing something intimate. Were they mating, or just passing food? In *Birds of Prey of Australia*, Stephen Debus writes, 'In courtship and when provisioning the incubating or brooding female, the male delivers prey in an aerial food-pass.' Perhaps there are chicks out there now. I will try not to project anything platitudinal upon this about endings and beginnings. More, I think about what felt right about passive observation – my dad and I in awe of the smoke hawk. Humans and birds coexisting. All temporary visitors.

Angela Meyer's debut novel, *A Superior Spectre*, was shortlisted for five literary awards in Australia and the UK. She won the inaugural Mslexia Novella Competition (UK) for *Joan Smokes*, and has released a book of flash fiction, *Captives*, and edited an anthology of spooky Australian stories, *The Great Unknown*. She is also a well-respected editor.

Georgina Steytler

Melanie Cheng

Looking up

It's stage three of the COVID-19 restrictions in Victoria. That elastic thing we call time has been stretched to its absolute limit. Days feel like weeks and the springtime stroll I took with my children along the banks of the Merri Creek seems like a distant memory.

In fact it was sometime in October, a mere five months ago. Before the virus. Before the closures. Before the run on toilet paper and hand sanitiser. Back when we could still kiss a friend to say hello. Back when we could still look forward to a night out at the theatre to see a sold-out show. Back when we were so busy we needed a smartphone to keep track of our activities. It was a rich, if at times exhausting, existence.

This particular outing was prompted by an IMAX documentary called *Backyard Wilderness* – a timely movie, which reminded us to take notice of the complex world beyond the four walls of our house. Feeling inspired, my children and I decided to visit the creek, only that day instead of whizzing by on our bikes and scooters, we would take our time, explore a little. Like the kids in the movie, we would examine all things and all spaces, including that much neglected area above our heads.

Within minutes of our departure, my son spotted a nest with three baby birds noisily awaiting the return of their mother. Used to his curiosity being rewarded, he was not surprised by his discovery, but I was. I hadn't expected the gratification to be so swift. Only that morning, as I'd enthused loudly about

Wayne Suffield

our expedition – a performance for my benefit as much as the kids' – I'd secretly braced myself for boredom, disappointment, tears.

Back when I was learning to scuba-dive, my instructor compared snorkelling to watching television and scuba diving to being inside the TV. That day at the creek, I remembered this analogy. As my children and I spied ladybirds in the grass and counted furry caterpillars on the trees, I realised that most of my adult life had been spent skimming the surface of things. I thought back to my first dive – the immersive wonder of it, the dreamlike novelty of breathing underwater. My intoxication with the remoteness and otherworldliness of that landscape had blinded me to the magic still to be found on land, in the long grass and the ancient trees.

It was their call that gave them away. A high-pitched crescendo-decrescendo cry, equal parts urgent and playful. I picked up my son and together we peered into the shadowy canopy of eucalypts, searching for a source. We didn't see them straight away – their dark feathers made them difficult to spot – but our eyes eventually found their bulky black bodies amid a curtain of crescent-shaped leaves.

It was their call that gave them away. A high-pitched crescendo-decrescendo cry, equal parts urgent and playful.

It was my, and my children's, introduction to the yellow-tailed black-cockatoo. The first thing that struck me was their size (the members of this particular flock were all at least the length of my forearm). The second thing was their colouring. They'd been blessed with that most stunning of combinations normally reserved for insects and frogs – an aposematic yellow and black. The markings, too, were a surprise. An eclectic mix of clownish cheeks and luxurious, lemon-yellow tails.

214

We stood at that lush bend of creek for a long time, watching the birds seek refuge in the cool shade of a gum tree. My kids, who ordinarily have short attention spans, were entranced. Later that night, I would read how the cockatoos' style of flying has been described by some observers as 'lazy', and how the English naturalist George Shaw initially named the species *Psittacus funereus* for its funereal colouring. As I lay in bed, I would think such comparisons unfair. Watching the flock take flight that warm October morning, their movements were more elegant than sluggish, and I would have sooner compared their inky feathers to a slick cocktail frock than some sombre funeral attire. But perhaps even in 1794, humans were more impressed with speed and flamboyance than a quiet, understated elegance.

Now that an invisible pathogen has forced human beings into hibernation, I imagine those yellow-cheeked cockatoos, soaring high above the empty streets and abandoned playgrounds, their unmistakable cries slicing through the suddenly unpolluted air – no longer having to compete with the hum of traffic or the drone of a plane or the beat of a jackhammer – and such imaginings offer some solace during these dark days and long nights.

If those magnificent creatures have taught me anything, it's that when life isn't looking up, that's exactly what we should do. Because who knows, we just may discover the answers – and if not the answers then at least a long-forgotten sense of wonder – in that much neglected space above our heads.

Melanie Cheng is a writer and general practitioner based in Melbourne. Her debut short story collection, *Australia Day*, won the 2018 Victorian Premier's Literary Award for Fiction. Her debut novel, *Room for a Stranger*, was shortlisted for the 2020 Multicultural NSW Award and longlisted for the 2020 Miles Franklin Literary Award. Her non-fiction has appeared in the *Age*, the *Australian*, SBS Online, *Meanjin*, *Overland* and *Griffith Review*, among others.

Wayne Suffield

Antoinette Roe

Me and the burrowing bees

A friend of mine was talking about these bees one day and I was listening to her go on about them. I thought, wait a minute, I know these bees. So I said, 'I know what bees you are talking about, and I know where they are.'

When I was a kid, we used to ride our horses down to the beach. We thought these humungous bees were dangerous, so we would bypass them and cut through the sand dunes so we wouldn't be stung. The buzzing was loud enough to scare anyone, you could hear them for miles. We would gallop through the dunes as fast as we could so that they wouldn't come after us.

I spoke to Gran Maureen Dodd about them. She told me the bees come out when the bluebells and poverty bush are in flower, so that they can go about their business.

These big hairy bees are only found on the claypans of the Gascoyne. One of the world's largest bee species, they are so remarkable they featured in David Attenborough's Life series a number of years ago.

The burrowing bee is also known as mungurragurra or sometimes jurrabarri in the Yinggarda language. The bees' larvae are a source of sweet food for Aboriginal people, many of whom speak with reverence about the bee and with fondness for the food it gives them.

The males are smaller and brown. The females make their burrows in the ground after it rains. Sometimes they clean out and reuse old burrows from years ago, coming back to their old grounds year after year. Sometimes there

Antoinette Roe

are thousands of burrows covering a red-soil claypan. Each little grub grows in a pool of honey in a capsule below the ground.

These bees are a delicacy to the Aboriginal people of the Gascoyne. After a month or two they will dig them up, cook them in their mud capsule in an open fire, knock the top off the capsule and eat them. The honey makes them sweet and buttery. They taste better than a lolly.

This was a story that needed to be told, so, with the assistance of the Fremantle-based film project Indigenous Community Stories, and Gwoonwardu Mia's – the Gascoyne Aboriginal Heritage and Cultural Centre's – exhibition team, we camped for a week out in the Gascoyne region with Aboriginal Elders, recording stories not only about the bee, but many other topics.

The final burrowing bee production features Indigenous Elders speaking about mungurragurra's traditional significance and the way to prepare its larvae for food. These are contemporary stories demonstrating ongoing connection to land and culture, and teaching the younger generations. The burrowing bee has become a significant exhibit at Gwoonwardu Mia. Visitors are first introduced to the story of the bee and its unusual nature, then encouraged to travel to locations around Carnarvon where they can actually view the bee for themselves.

The buzzing was loud enough to scare anyone, you could hear them for miles. We would gallop through the dunes as fast as we could so that they wouldn't come after us.

One day I went for a drive to see if the bees were out.

I got there all excited, expecting to see a few bees buzzing around. To my disappointment there was nothing. I got out of the car and walked up and down the road for a while to see if there was any sign of the bees, but zilch.

I was about to walk back to the car when I saw something on the side of the road. I bent down to see what it was and, to my surprise, it was a lifeless bee. I carefully wrapped him up in tissue and put him gently in the console of the car and drove back to work.

The next day Gran Maureen and I went out to Pelican Point to see if there was anything happening with the bees. We discovered two fresh burrows and one lonely bee flying around. We were over the moon because we knew that within a week or so there would be more and more bees each day.

Four days later, Mum, Alice and I went back to Pelican Point. As we came over the rise, Mum and I screamed when we saw the road full of burrows, and hundreds of bees flying around. It gave us the biggest adrenaline rush ever.

The next morning, we rose with the beautiful warmth of the sun. It was time to put the kettle on and have a few cuppas before heading to the Kennedy Ranges.

We drove into the claypan hoping to find it full of burrowing bees, but there was nothing. We drove back to Coona to pack up our things and start our long journey to Wooramel Station to camp for the night.

That night we talked about the emu in the Milky Way and had a good laugh.

At Meedo Station we were welcomed with open arms. After slipping and sliding over a claypan, and one of the cars getting bogged, we saw a couple of bees flying around. We stopped to check them out. There were two males fighting. I'm not sure what they were fighting about because there were no females around at the time. I got out and took a few photos. We drove a little further and stopped to stretch our legs.

There in the distance were bees in their hundreds.

Wow, what a sight!

We were so happy that we had finally found the bees after driving hundreds of kilometres to track them down. We prepared a fire and chucked the billy on to boil water for a cuppa. Cakes and scones were also on the menu. After morning tea, we set out armed with cameras, careful not to step on the bees or their burrows.

Our job was done. It was time to head back to Gwoonwardu Mia. We arrived back home safe and sound and all exhausted, but we had had the best time of our lives.

They wanted to film me as well. I was filmed at Tuckers Pump as part of a story on the bees. This can be seen in the interpretive exhibition at Gwoonwardu Mia in Carnarvon, Western Australia.

220

Antoinette Roe works for the Gwoonwardu Mia cultural centre. She is an artist who has been commissioned to create public artworks, a member of the local Aboriginal weaving group, and a defender and promoter of burrowing bees. She lives in Carnarvon.

Linda Rogan

Nayuka
Gorrie

Nanwan

Naming is powerful. It carries an omnipotence that I take seriously. When I found out I was pregnant, one of my first undertakings was to choose a name. I loved my name growing up, never once anglicised it and was proud that every time I said it out loud, I was speaking my language. I wanted the same for my children.

The Royal Women's Hospital stands shoulder to shoulder with the Royal Melbourne Hospital. They even share a food court. In early November 2018, my father passed away at the Royal Melbourne Hospital. In late November 2019, I gave birth to twins at the Royal Women's Hospital, at twenty-seven weeks. I decided to name my firstborn children something that would honour my late father; something that would tether us together in his absence. Dad was a Collingwood supporter and this support is something I've inherited, so I decided to find out what magpies are called in Mum's language, Gunaikurnai. I hoped it would be beautiful, lyrical and strong. Instead it had a guttural sound – glart or klart. It goes without saying, I love my language and my people, but I was not going to name my children glart or klart. Mum later sent me a message with the word nanwan – the magpie lark. I loved the way this looked, and I liked saying it. The only problem was I didn't know much about these birds.

Magpie larks are often mistaken for magpies. They are smaller, and have no relation to magpies or larks. I have always found their tiny bills elegant and their small head–big body combination very cute. Aside from this, I felt

Wayne Suffield

a connection and thought of them as unremarkable and common. Suddenly, like a word you've learnt for the first time, I started seeing them everywhere – on my street, outside our local café, in carparks.

The elevators on level four of the Royal Women's open up to a small garden framed by windows and glass doors. Here, nurses sit around in groups eating their leftovers, or alone, hunched over, staring vacantly at their phones. Women recovering from their caesarean sections sit slumped in wheelchairs, long white elastic stockings hugging their legs to prevent blood clots. In the background, you can hear bewildered fathers happy-shout down their phones.

After hours of breathing recycled air, the garden is always a reprieve. Yet, for several days over the course of our months in the Neonatal Intensive Care Unit, I couldn't go outside. The city was smothered by noxious smoke drifting across from the Gippsland bushfires, ravaging my country, my children's country. I tried not to think that I was breathing in my country's corpse, but the image kept haunting me. I wondered what world I had brought the twins into and what would still be left of their country by the time they were allowed to visit it.

I often imagine the cement and tar and bitumen suffocating the land. On top of concrete and glass and metal, someone decided to make a garden in a hospital. Often, while I was there, out of the corner of my eye I would see little birds flitting around, making do. Making a home out of what they could.

After my babies left their first home inside my body, we made the best of our home at the hospital, inside the NICU. I began to get to know the twins, Nanwan and Yeerung. I

The nanwan survives

across the continent,

in cities and in the bush

and everywhere

in between.

watched them flit between being intubated and ventilated, to CPAP, back to intubation and so on down the oxygen support ladder. I spent hundreds of hours by their side watching the effort of breathing, waiting for their lungs to get stronger and bigger. While the fires raged, while we missed the Invasion Day march, I pondered what it meant to raise black children in a colonised country. I wondered how long we would remain two kilometres from Melbourne's CBD. When would the kids see a tree or hear a bird? How could they flourish when I couldn't imagine a life beyond travelling between Brunswick and Parkville?

It has been so long since I've spent any time on country that I am even excited by the sight of grass. There are weeds sprouting among my kale and spring onions – I am so desperate for living things, I will take anything. I am not in a position right now to be a purist or elitist in terms of the nature I appreciate. There are two slugs that have taken up residence in my bathroom. They appear in the shower sometime after eleven pm and disappear sometime before four am. This time last year I would have demanded their eviction, but now it's nice to share those quiet minutes with them. Who am I to decide it's not their home?

This is the longest I have ever spent in the city. I can't even remember the last time I saw the Birrarung River. While my two babies were in the NICU from November 2019 to March 2020, the only time I felt fresh air on my sun-deprived skin was in the thirty seconds it took to get from the front door to our car. We travelled for fifteen minutes along Royal Parade, following the tram tracks to the Royal Women's Hospital and then back home at the end of the day.

We would pass by nanwans on a patch of grass down a backstreet. Even when smoke covered the scorched and suffocating land, they would be enjoying themselves, eating, and occasionally fighting another bird. Nanwans do well in urban environments but can also be found outside the city. Their population is stable. Our continent has the highest rate of language extinction, and there are close to 2000 at-risk plants and animals, yet among all this the nanwan thrives.

My Nanwan is thriving too. Four weeks ago, they came off their last oxygen support mechanism – low flow. Last week they started rolling. They look me in the eyes and babble. I still don't know when they will see their country. I know their country will welcome them with warm open arms, and in the meantime, we are making a home with what we have. The nanwan survives across the continent, in cities and in the bush and everywhere in between. Their ability to adapt helps them make a home anywhere, but they live on my country too. In this, I hope my own Nanwan lives up to their name.

Nayuka Gorrie is a Gunai, Gunditjmara, Wiradjuri and Yorta Yorta writer. Nayuka's work spans social commentary and features for publications such as the *Saturday Paper*, the *Guardian*, the *Lifted Brow* and *NITV*, and television writing for *Black Comedy* and *Get Krack!n*. They have featured in *Queerstories*, *Going Postal: More than 'Yes' or 'No'* and the *Growing Up Queer in Australia* anthology. They are a recipient of the Wheeler Centre's Next Chapter scheme. Nayuka is writing a book of essays exploring contemporary colonialism.

Maia Loeffler

A language of clicks

A deep purple bleeds across the horizon. The gravel crunches beneath our feet as we walk through the low-lit park towards the canopy of ageing trees. I am fourteen, and still scared of the dark. I cling close to my mother, burying my hand with hers in her coat pocket. We stop in a clearing near the edge of a gloomy lake and look up at the trees. We wait in silence. A black shape flits swiftly across the sky, the flapping sound of its wings slicing through the night air. It lands with a loud rustle into the tree above us. Another follows; two, three, four more glide and settle into the same ficus. Bats. We listen as they chirp and shriek at the sight of their bounty. My eyes strain to see them, and for the first time ever, I forget my fear and let the night engulf me, listening to their strange but intriguing noises. They speak in a language of clicks, a tongue so foreign.

The park will wake at dawn to a floor littered with leftovers and unwanted scraps – I wake with a new-found love of bats.

I met Julie's bats at JABS (Joey and Bat Sanctuary) five years later, on a cold, overcast day – the kind of Melbourne weather that makes you want to wear a coat indoors. I had been to her house before, having sewn pouches for her joeys when I should have been studying for my year twelve exams. But this time, after enduring three anti-rabies injections in a row, I was ready to meet the bats.

Vivien Jones

After the ten am feeding of tiny kangaroos and sugar gliders, Julie led me to the corner of the room, where a basket full of blankets lay resting on the couch. Nestled in the middle was Zach, wheezing from a tube attached to a ventilator on the table nearby. An eighteen-day-old grey-headed flying fox, who had been found lying on the side of a road, Zach now had severe pneumonia. The only muscle moving was his abdomen, which quivered with each breath. Julie said not to get my hopes up, as it was unlikely he would make it to the following week.

But when I walked in the door a week later, I was hit with a chorus of ear-splitting screeches. Not only was Zach alive and recovering well, the wails coming from his spot in the basket were joined by those of some newly rescued bats – Mum and Pup – who were cuddling in a temporary pen on the kitchen bench. Mum and Pup had been found in someone's garage, hanging off a treadmill.

Each week that summer more and more bats arrived at Julie's sanctuary after being found heat-stressed, some on the verge of death. I learnt to swaddle the babies up in their 'mama rolls' (fabric that emulates the feeling of clinging on to their mothers, being wrapped in their warm wings). I was taught how to bottle-feed them carefully, holding them at the exact right angle so milk would not spew out their noses. I soon discovered that what I thought were claws were actually just exceptionally sharp thumbs, and I learnt the hard way not to let them anywhere near my face.

The living room was soon transformed into a jungle gym for bats, a wooden structure that they could hang upside down from to their hearts' content. The older bats were kept outside in 'creche', an aviary, where they could shriek loudly and flap their wings without knocking over photo frames and remote controls.

And before long, I had fallen in love with bats, their velvet wings, their fragile fingers. Their curious eyes and love-heart noses. Their distinct personalities and chirps of disgust, happiness, impatience, fear. I began to understand Zach and what he meant by 'trrrrrrr' (a long chirp meant 'feed me', a shorter one meant 'I'm about to climb on your face and scratch you'). I held a special place in my heart for Zach, who I had seen transform from a weak, dying pup to a determined, stubborn teen. He liked my hair, which happened to be the same colour as his fur. Climbing into my light-brown ponytail for camouflage, he would claw his thumbs into my ears to keep his balance. I was there for his first flap of wings, which happened while we were sunning outside, Zach hanging from my collar. I saw his first body-lift, where he swayed the upper part of his torso from side to side. I felt I could tell what he was thinking: he wanted to fly. And I was there for his first take-off and crashlanding, right into a basket of dirty washing.

The grey-headed flying fox is native to the east coast of Australia, stretching from northern Queensland all the way down to Melbourne, even found in Adelaide at times. They are the only flying fox endemic to Australia. Melbourne has a permanent colony, and if you are lucky enough to be there at sunset, the gum trees come alive with thousands of waking bats. They take to the sky at dusk, flying up to fifty kilometres to feeding areas. In the spring and summer months, one gum tree is left as a designated nursery, where babysitter bats are tasked to watch over the juveniles while their parents go out to dine.

I soon learn that the morning 'litter' that graces my local park is evidence of successful pollination and seed dispersal, which our native trees rely on so heavily. Grey-headed flying foxes are responsible for so much of the regeneration and growth of Australia's forests. We often associate these creatures with bloodsucking vampires, while, in reality, the only blood spilt is their own. Habitat clearing and rising temperatures are making these misunderstood creatures extremely vulnerable – and the consequences are already revealing themselves. If numbers continue to decline, our native flora will suffer immensely, decreasing in richness and abundance across Australia. This makes Julie, and many other brave wildlife carers, more important than ever.

I return to the park on warm nights, no longer needing to wrap myself in my mother's wings. As twilight ripples across the sky, the bats gradually join me. Creatures of the dark, they bring the joy of the wild to my ordinary urban existence.

Maia Loeffler grew up surrounded by a menagerie – dogs, cats, axolotls, rabbits – and is an avid nature lover. She is currently studying a Bachelor of Science, majoring in zoology, at the University of Melbourne, with a year of cross-institutional studies at the University of Western Australia. Maia is a passionate macro photographer, scuba diver, artist and writer. She won the 2015 La Trobe University Young Writers' Award and in 2018 was shortlisted for the National Gallery of Victoria's Top Arts.

Bruce Pascoe

Binyaroo

I have seen four powerful owls but heard a few hundred, I have seen six owlet-nightjars but only three at roost, I have seen a thousand gliding white-throated nightjars but only five on the ground. The rarity is explained by the night but also by their small populations, and yet their beings are stapled to my heart. I feel the hooks twinge in my flesh every time they appear. Each is a mythic animal, and all are spirit beings for Aboriginal Australians.

The cormorant, on the other hand, is as common as a foam cup in a gutter and so easily dismissed by humans. Its bland everydayness, its oiliness and goat-like croakiness seem to make it invisible to most people.

But the little black cormorant is among my favourite animals. I am enthralled by them. On six occasions I have seen them sweep into a small inlet on the salty Wallagaraugh–Genoa river system, as fearsome and dreaded as any fighter squadron.

The mob of thirty-three – their numbers have barely changed over the last fifty years – veers into a lagoon in tight formation over the heads of five or six patient pelicans, who seem to have been awaiting the arrival of the amphibious platoon. The cormorants dive in a serried rank across the surface and the water erupts with panicked fish as they are driven into a pincer towards the shore. Once embayed, the fish leap and surge in desperation, and the cormorants take full toll of this while the pelicans glide in decorous calm to scoop up any fish that escape the cordon of cormorants.

Michael Livingston

Michael Livingston

The last time I was witness to this operation a white egret took up a strategic position on the bank, and snipped up any little fish that flung itself into the air to avoid capture. The operation was clinical and three different bird species worked in concert.

The next day I saw the same cormorant fishing fleet and in the space of half an hour both the white egret and two of the pelican flock flew over them. I wonder if the three species acknowledged each other and the success of their campaign the previous day. They seemed so aware of each other's roles in the operation and both the pelican and egret were so clearly awaiting the arrival of air support that I cannot believe they wouldn't look at each other with the memory acknowledged between them. A fishing conspiracy.

I don't want to demean their behaviour by comparing it to ours, but neither do I want to underrate their intelligence, to separate myself from them. I want to be one of them, just another sentient animal living on the river.

Bruce Pascoe is a Yuin and Tasmanian man who lives in East Gippsland. A board member of the Aboriginal Corporation for Languages, he has written over thirty books spanning fiction, non-fiction and children's titles. He was awarded the Prime Minister's Literary Award for *Fog a Dox* in 2012, and received the prestigious Australia Council Award for Lifetime Achievement in Literature in 2018. *Dark Emu*, a history of Aboriginal agriculture, was published by Magabala in 2014 and won Book of the Year in the 2016 NSW Premier's Literary Awards, with Bruce co-winning the Indigenous Writers' Prize. *Dark Emu* was performed by Bangarra Dance Theatre in 2018. *Salt: Selected stories and essays* is his most recent book.

Patrick Tomkins

Photographers

Tim Bawden is an IT professional from Melbourne who spends his spare time exploring the natural world. His favourite place to be is out on a pelagic boat trip or spotlighting in the forests around Melbourne. A strong believer in the power of citizen science, Tim freely shares his photos and experiences to help shine a light on nature and the plight it faces.

Kristian Bell was born in the US but raised on the island of Jersey in the UK. Despite having been a keen nature lover his whole life, Kristian held numerous 'sensible' jobs (data analyst, investment strategist, general manager of a private jet charter company) before returning to his passion for the natural world. He is currently nearing completion of a PhD at Deakin University, investigating the ecology of spinifex grass in agricultural landscapes, with the aim of improving the abundance and condition of this iconic Australian plant.

Rohan Bilney grew up in eastern Victoria with a fascination for nature. After completing a science degree in Melbourne, he returned home to complete an honours degree and PhD investigating the ecology of large forest owls and small mammal decline since European settlement. He is particularly interested in threatened species in forested ecosystems, and currently lives and works as an ecologist in southern New South Wales.

Justin Bruhn is an award-winning underwater photographer based on the Sunshine Coast in Queensland. Many of his images were captured on the Great Barrier Reef, where he spends as much time underwater behind his camera as possible. His love for the ocean inspires him to connect people to the beauty of our endangered marine life, and to raise awareness of marine conservation through his artwork. More of Justin's work can be viewed on his website, www.pureunderwaterimaging.com.

Andrew Buckle is a nature photographer and gastroenterologist from Melbourne. He loves watching and photographing endangered Australian birds, and has a particular interest in parrots and black-cockatoos. He is passionate about all aspects of animal and plant conservation, and is a member of BirdLife Australia, Zoos Victoria and the Victorian National Parks Association. He is also a keen scuba diver, sea-slug enthusiast and St Kilda Pier penguin guide.

Matt Clancy is a Melbourne-based ecologist and wildlife photographer specialising in the incredible world of herpetology (reptiles and amphibians). Matt is currently employed as a research assistant at the University of Melbourne, working to save endangered frogs, as well as on various frog-related bioacoustic projects. Matt will continue to travel across Australia (and abroad) photographing and documenting the natural history of frogs, reptiles, and an assortment of other wildlife in their natural habitats.

Dr Amy Coetsee is a threatened-species biologist at Zoos Victoria, fighting the extinction of some of Victoria's most endangered species. She has a strong background in conservation, research, government policy and science communication. Amy currently leads several recovery projects, specialising in eastern barred bandicoots, where she has over fifteen years of experience. She is involved in all aspects of eastern barred bandicoot conservation, including planning, monitoring, research, threat mitigation and community engagement.

Craig Coverdale is a Sydney-based urban landscape photographer.

Angus Emmott is a third-generation beef cattle producer in Western Queensland. He has always been passionate about biology, natural resource management and photography. His goal on his family property is to attempt to work with nature, which includes leaving the dingo population alone.

Jayne Jenkins is an award-winning underwater photographer. She has worked as a safety diver and researcher for film, television and photographic expeditions, including the cave-diving spectacular *Sanctum*, *Chasing Coral* and an upcoming documentary about seahorses for the BBC. Jayne was inducted into the Women Divers Hall of Fame, is a fellow of the Explorers Club, and in 2020 was chosen to be one of ten Ocean Science Champions for the United Nations Decade of Ocean Science for Sustainable Development. For the past fourteen years she has also mentored countless scholars as Vice President of the Our World Underwater Scholarship Society.

Vivien Jones is a photographer and the author of *Flying Foxes: Australian night foresters*. Over the past thirty years Vivien has raised dozens of orphaned flying foxes and cared for adult bats in distress. She has taken a particular interest in the return of these animals to the wild, and has worked alongside scientists as a photographer, documenting the behaviour of individual animals. She hopes her work will help foster a better understanding of animal behaviour.

Sue Liu is an author, artist and diver. She films, writes about and illustrates Australian sea and land critters, under the name Wildcard-Sue.

Michael Livingston is a health researcher, book lover, birdwatcher and amateur photographer based in Melbourne. He spends his spare time tramping through the city's parks taking photos of birds.

Caleb McElrea is a science communicator, wildlife photographer and filmmaker living in Melbourne. The highland rainforests of the Scenic Rim in Queensland were the backdrop for most of his childhood getaways and instilled in him a resilient love for and connection with the natural world. He started photographing wildlife when he was in his early teens, and recently graduated with first-class honours in zoology from the University of Melbourne.

Nick Monaghan is a wildlife photographer who specialises in capturing images of Australia's incredibly diverse insects and spiders, as well as its stunning native wildflowers. His website, www.lifeunseen.com, is dedicated to his passion for macro photography and offers galleries containing thousands of photos of nature's living works of art.

Dr Richard Pillans is a research scientist with CSIRO Oceans and Atmosphere. His research focuses on the movement and population dynamics of various marine species, including fish, sharks, turtles and dugong. Much of his research is on threatened species, with a focus on improving our understanding of how human activities such as fishing and habitat modification influence population status. Richard is also a keen underwater photographer.

Gillian Rayment developed an interest in wildlife during her teens when she began to paint our feathered friends, inspired by her own photography. Over the years she has won numerous awards, and her passion is still as strong as ever. She has also self-published a book featuring the superb blue wrens of Kangaroo Island (*Vivonne Bay Blue*), and a DVD (*Wings Above – Island Below*) about Kangaroo Island's natural splendour.

Linda Rogan has been editor of the *Victorian Entomologist* since 2010. After retiring as a physiotherapist and manager in aged care in 2002, she had time to really pursue her interests. These moved from flora – native orchids in particular – to pollinators and insects that are attracted to the indigenous plants in her garden. Australian native bees are one of her special interests.

David Maurice Smith is a Canadian photographer and director currently based in Sydney. In 2016 he was awarded a grant from the Pulitzer Center on Crisis Reporting for his work chronicling a suicide epidemic in the remote Canadian First Nations community of Attawapiskat, Ontario. His images have been recognised in the International Photography Awards, the American Photography Awards and the Amnesty International Media Awards, and in 2016 he received a Walkley Award for his photographic coverage of the European refugee crisis.

Steve Smith is a Professor of Marine Science at Southern Cross University's National Marine Science Centre. He is passionate about marine biodiversity and its conservation, and uses photography to foster broader appreciation and understanding of Australia's amazing marine organisms. Steve is particularly interested in the bizarre and colourful sea slugs, and works closely with citizen scientists to photographically document their diversity and distribution in the Australasian region.

Colin Southwell is an ecologist who has researched wild animal populations in remote regions of the world, from outback Australia to Antarctica. In the past twenty-five years he has participated in fifteen research expeditions to Antarctica, studying seal, penguin and seabird populations to identify and ameliorate threats from climate change, fisheries and human activities. His time with crabeater seals in the remote pack ice of the Southern Ocean is a career highlight.

Georgina Steytler was the first Australian woman to win a category (Behaviour: Invertebrates) in Wildlife Photographer of the Year, the world's foremost nature photography competition. She was the Grand Prix Winner of the EAAFP Waterbirds Photo Contest, the winner of the 2017 Bird Photographer of the Year competition (Creative Imagery) and the 2017 Australian Photography Awards (Wildlife), and the 2016 Australian Geographic Nature Photographer of the Year (Portfolio Prize).

Wayne Suffield is a former English and Media teacher of thirty-five years. He is a wildlife and landscape photographer, predominantly in the Ararat district. Birds in flight are his particular passion, and his mission is to reveal the remarkable nature and skills of birds, capturing their nuance and micro-movements.

Heather Sutton is a leading firefighter and underwater photographer. She has dived extensively in Australia, as well as in Fiji, the Philippines, Papua New Guinea and Timor-Leste, among other destinations. She has a particular interest in sharks and wrecks.

Peter Taylor is a Brisbane-based photographer and birder. He has had an interest in bird behaviour from a young age, which he has developed through painting and photography. Peter enjoys blurring the boundary between landscape and portraiture, and his images have been featured in *Australian Geographic* and other nature publications.

William Terry is a zoological researcher with Southern Cross University and an environment officer for the Macedon Ranges Shire Council, where he works to conserve brush-tailed phascogales in their natural habitat. In his spare time he is an enthusiastic wildlife photographer, always chasing the next challenging species.

Dr Patrick Tomkins has a background in ecotoxicology, but after a brief stint in academia he realised he was happiest when out in the field. He now works as a field ecologist, surveying rare and threatened fauna throughout Australia. This allows him to pursue his other passion – wildlife photography. There is something very special about sharing a secret moment with an animal, and he tries to capture that in his photos.

Matt Wright runs wildlife tour business Faunagraphic in South East Queensland. He is an aspiring naturalist, wildlife photographer and wildlife rehabilitator who has had an interest in fauna from a young age.

Acknowledgements

So many wonderful people lent their passionate support to this project. Our deepest gratitude to the awesome team at PRH – Meredith Curnow, Melissa Lane, Nikla Martin, Catherine Hill, James Rendall, Lou Ryan, Justin Ractliffe, Julie Burland, Lucy Ballantyne and Gavin Schwarcz – who went above and beyond the call of duty to produce such a beautiful book. We are grateful to Jay Labzin and Ingrid Neilson from the Australian Marine Conservation Society and Tim Allard and Heather Paterson from Australian Wildlife Conservancy for their assistance. Special thanks to Alon Loeffler for helping create the early vision behind this book.